ROBERT DE NIRO

MOVIE TOP TEN

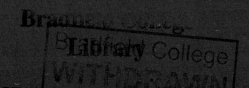

CREDITS

ROBERT DE NIRO: MOVIE TOP TEN
Edited by Jack Hunter
ISBN 1 871592 88 7
© Creation Books & individual contributors 1999
Creation Movie Top Tens: a periodical, review-based publication
First published 1999 by:
Creation Books International
Design/layout/typesetting:
Bradley Davis, PCP International
Cover illustration:
"Taxi Driver"

Photo credits:
All photos are authorised publicity stills, by courtesy of the BFI, London; Museum Of Modern Art, New York; and the Jack Hunter Collection.

Copyright acknowledgements:
Every reasonable effort has been made to trace the owners of copyright materials in this book, but in some instances this has proven impossible. The editor and publishers will be glad to receive information leading to more complete acknowledgements in subsequent printings of the book, and in the meantime extend their apologies for any omissions.

British Library Cataloguing in Publication Data:
A catalogue record for this book is available from the British Library

A Butcherbest Production

Creation Books
"Popular books for popular people"

CONTENTS

INTRODUCTION
"PERFORMING MIRACLES"
NOTES ON A LIFE
IN SCREEN ACTING

There's a story, possibly apocryphal, concerning the poorly received but somewhat undervalued 1994 film, **Mary Shelley's Frankenstein**. During pre-production rehearsals, the actor playing the Creature was preoccupied with finding a suitably grotesque look for his monstrous character. Eventually, he gave his director and co-star – Kenneth Branagh – some photographs of murder victims, taken at the scene of the crime, moments after the discovery of the brutally ruined corpses. Already nervous thanks to the daunting scale of the production, Branagh was a little disturbed by the content of the pictures. Then he noticed the date printed on the rear of the 8 x 10s. The photos had been taken only two days previously. "Where the fuck did you get these?" he inquired, astonished. His leading man shrugged and muttered in a matter-of-fact fashion, "I know a guy..."

It's easy to believe the story is true. Robert De Niro had played timid crime scene photographer Wayne Dobie in John McNaughton's **Mad Dog And Glory** a year before. The actor had spent time with real forensics officers, so it's entirely feasible that he may have had unique access to such gruesome material. For a time, it seemed as if that was how history would remember Robert De Niro: not for his skill and range as an actor, but for the obsessive detail with which he researched each role.

This was the man who learned the entire Roman Catholic mass – in Latin – before he could feel comfortable in the garments of duplicitous priest Des Spellacy in **True Confessions** (1981). For **The Untouchables** (1987), he insisted on having silk underwear made in the same store from which his character, Al Capone, purchased his luxurious lingerie. There's even a ridiculous myth surrounding the depth of his research into mob activity for **Goodfellas**, far too incredible, and libelous, to repeat here. Most famously of course, he piled on the pounds to play a bloated Jake La Motta in **Raging Bull**, but only after contesting a few semi-pro bouts as the boxer's younger incarnation. Such extreme behaviour always impresses the Academy, and De Niro duly collected his only Best Actor Oscar to date (he'd won in the Supporting category for **The Godfather Part II**, in 1974). In the case of **Raging Bull**, he contributed something more than a compelling performance. He and Scorsese reworked the early screenplay drafts by Paul Schrader and

Mardik Martin – deemed unfilmable by United Artists studio executives – to get beneath La Motta's skin and showing the man inside the beast.[1]

MOGUL AND HIRED HAND

Towards the end of the 1980s, De Niro's working methods changed considerably. It was at this time that he established the Tribeca centre, named for the area of New York in which it was situated. Part studio, part facilities house, part creative haven, the idea behind Tribeca was to create a hive of movie activity on the East coast, away from the pernicious influence of Hollywood and the more artificial atmosphere of the California lifestyle. Although the venture attracted many high profile investors, among them Martin Scorsese, Danny De Vito, and Bill Murray, De Niro was the figurehead and largest single contributor. He began to increase his workload to fund Tribeca. In the first two decades of his screen career, the actor made on average twelve films. In the '90s he has made thirty. Obviously, shooting three films a year put an end to such practices as spending four months gorging on pasta or learning ring craft. (Daniel Day Lewis has probably seized the method crown in that respect.) Critical convention has it that this has diluted De Niro's talent, and there's no doubt that the likes of **Backdraft** and **Great Expectations** do his filmography few favours, but I would argue that this has been a hugely productive period for the star. By working continuously, he has built up an impressive body of work and become a far more versatile and relaxed actor. It's not that his later performances are in any way *better* than those in **Taxi Driver** or **The Deer Hunter**, from a period when a new De Niro picture was an event, it's just that we get to enjoy his work on different levels, take pleasure in watching him for different reasons.

COP, CROOK, DOCTOR

Witness 1997. In twelve short months he appeared in **Jackie Brown**, **Copland**, and **Wag The Dog**. The first two performances were supporting roles, admittedly, but they were vital to the success of the respective pictures. Crucially they also involved being guided by two young writer-directors, hip auteurs only recently emerged from the independent film making community. In James Mangold's **Copland**, the actor is called upon to show remarkable subtlety in his depiction of Internal Affairs officer Moe Tilden. He should be the film's moral centre, yet even he is compromised when manipulating Sylvester Stallone's slow-witted sheriff into action. He gets one terrific speech in the process, bellowing at Stallone: "You had a chance to be a cop and you blew it."

Mary Shelley's Frankenstein

His work for Quentin Tarantino in **Jackie Brown** couldn't have been more different, as Louis Gara's stoned countenance transformed into a paranoid, psychotic grimace. Two terrific turns in minor parts, then, just as De Niro had contributed ten years earlier in the **Angel Heart/The Untouchables** sinister extended cameo double whammy, but in 1997 there was still time for a leading role in Barry Levinson's **Wag The Dog**. The film had strange origins: Levinson, De Niro and Dustin Hoffman had worked together the year before on the flawed drama **Sleepers** (in which De Niro has by far the best moment in the picture when being told of the abuse the young boys from his parish suffered. The audience doesn't get to hear the full horror, but De Niro is our conduit, as his eyes slowly fill with tears). All three enjoyed the experience and were keen to repeat it, but had only the smallest of windows in their schedules. Working from David Mamet's screenplay, they cast, shot and edited the political satire in thirteen weeks. In the '70s, De Niro would've spent that long deciding whether or not to do the film in the first place or, if he *had* committed, to undertaking his painstaking research process. Now he took on producing as well as acting duties on the project. (And as with

The Untouchables

the other two films, he worked for a reduced salary, giving the lie to the perceived notion of his having turned mercenary in the '90s). His performance as spin doctor Conrad Brean doesn't suffer from the enforced pace, if anything it benefits from the rough and ready style of the piece. In long, loose single takes, De Niro and Hoffman circle each other like tribal elders performing an ancient ritual, and the actor also seems invigorated by working opposite younger talents, such as Woody Harrelson and Anne Heche.

YOUNG BLOOD

Much of the actor's best work has come when sharing the screen with inexperienced co-stars. Think of the neighbourhood kids in **Sleepers**, or Lillo Brancato and Francis Capra in his directorial debut, **A Bronx Tale** (1993). Most of all, think of his electrifying clashes with Leonardo DiCaprio in **This Boy's Life** (1993 – another vintage year, with an against-type appearance in **Mad Dog And Glory** also in cinemas). Watching the two men go to war in the family kitchen represented everything that is great about the post-war

This Boy's Life

American movie acting tradition. All the groundwork done by Brando, Clift and Dean in the '50s came to fruition in those exchanges, and it's to be hoped DiCaprio's subsequent rise to global megastardom is never allowed to eclipse his talent. Low key the film may have been, and a box office flop, but its place in the annals of cinema is assured by the Bobby and Leo scenes alone. De Niro's eagerness to work with newcomers isn't a symptom of elder statesman status, where he gives his seal of approval to the next generation in exchange for a burst of energy or credibility. Instead it's a practice which dates back to **The Deer Hunter**, in 1978.

Since becoming a star in **The Godfather Part II**, the actor had made some conservative choices. He'd returned to Scorsese territory for **Taxi Driver** (1976 – another Oscar nomination and surprise box office success) and **New York, New York** (a disaster). There was also the rambling and unfocused **The Last Tycoon** (1976), which at least represented a chance to learn from one of the great directors, Elia Kazan. Bertolucci's **1900** meant working with one of the acknowledged giants of European art cinema. **The Deer Hunter** however, was the first film in which De Niro had the chance to exert significant influence of his own on the production as a whole. He it was who suggested (and when a star suggests, studios and second-time directors like

Michael Cimino treat it as a demand) stage actors Christopher Walken and Meryl Streep for the key roles as Nick and Linda. Walken picked up a Best Supporting Actor Oscar, and Streep's career received a kick start which soon saw her established as the most critically admired actress of the modern era.

The star also lined up alongside his director when the studio wanted cuts in the film's three hour running time. The creative forces won that particular battle, and **The Deer Hunter** went on to win Oscars for Best Picture and Director, with De Niro losing out to John Voight for Best Actor in that year's other "Vietnam" movie, **Coming Home**. There are those who will tell you that **The Deer Hunter** is at best ridiculous and at worst racist, but they're wrong, and by a long chalk. It is in fact a romantic epic, and has nothing to do with the war in South East Asia and everything to do with American Pastoral variations on mythic themes. It's also unbearably moving and exceptionally tense, and for this most of the credit must go to its star. Any auteurists out there protesting at the director's sacred right to authorship should sit through everything Michael Cimino has made since and then try to convince themselves that **The Deer Hunter** isn't truly Robert De Niro's triumph.

A BLESSED UNION

The Deer Hunter is not covered in depth in this collection, and while it's absence is regrettable, it is perhaps an inevitable consequence of the desire for as broad a cross section of movies as possible – to give a career overview, rather than a predictable selection of highlights. It would be remiss however to ignore this and certain other entries in the De Niro back catalogue. **Mean Streets** (1973) obviously merits more than a passing mention. Not only is it a fine picture in its own right (covered extensively in the *Harvey Keitel Movie Top Ten*, published earlier in this series), it is also significant as the first fruit of the most important actor/director partnership in film history. Indeed, it would've been very easy – and wholly justified – to virtually monopolise this book with the eight films De Niro has made with Martin Scorsese. In the end, **Taxi Driver, Raging Bull, King Of Comedy** and **Cape Fear** made the cut and there can be little argument with their selection, but the other collaborations are equally deserving of inclusion.

Shambolic though **New York, New York** may have been, at the very least it gave De Niro his first stab at a romantic lead, albeit a self-centred, insecure individual, but hey – that was the '70s. Better was to come when the two re-united after a seven year spell apart, post-**King Of Comedy**, to make **Goodfellas**. When we see Jimmy Conway working the room through the eyes of young hood Henry Hill, we understand the attraction of a life of crime. If a few truck hijacks can buy you this kind of charisma, who wants to

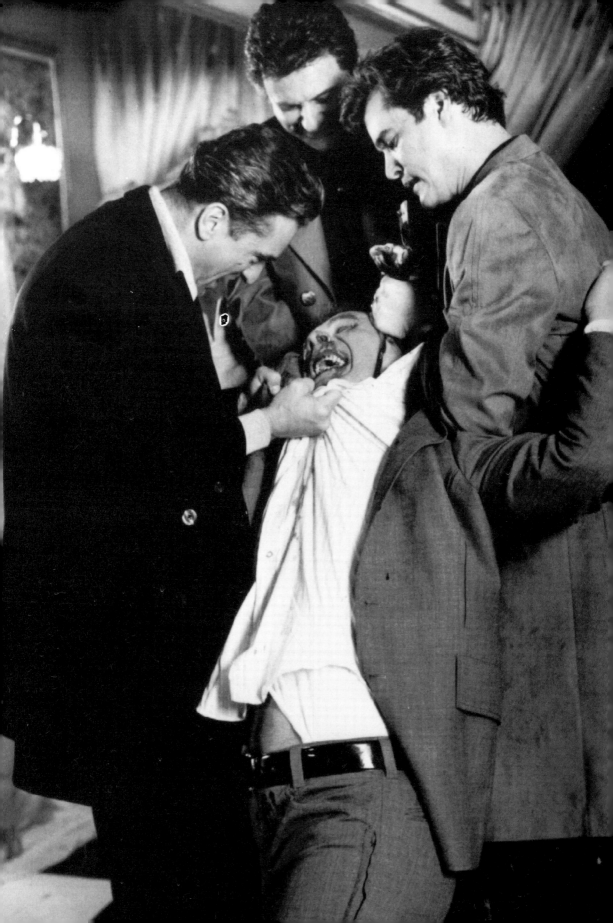

waste time among the ranks of the law-abiding? Jimmy's final fate, staring balefully at life imprisonment through an old man's bifocals are a reminder of the old adage that crime doesn't pay.

The pair followed that immediately with **Cape Fear**, with De Niro as the muscle bound, tattoo-adorned angel of vengeance Max Cady. Both may have made the film as a kind of experiment in commercial cinema, but that didn't stop them producing a superior thriller. It's unfortunate that Robert Redford, originally cast as De Niro's lawyer nemesis, bailed before shooting began. His replacement, Nick Nolte, possesses immense screen presence and is a fine actor, but he's nobody's idea of the embodiment of American ideals. With golden boy Redford up against him, De Niro might've had even more to sink his teeth into – and not just the flesh of the woman he brutalises.

The duo's last joint effort to date is **Casino**, a film actually criticised for being too similar to **Goodfellas**, as if that could ever be a bad thing. Here, as Ace Rothstein, De Niro is a paradox – a gambler and a control freak. He'll bet on horses, play the odds at a table, but insists on supervising his environment and relationships to an obsessive degree. Joe Pesci and Sharon Stone get to go spectacularly but effectively over the top as unhinged partner in crime and adulterous wife respectively, but it's De Niro's performance which anchors the entire film. **Casino** and Michael Mann's **Heat** were released within weeks of each other, giving audiences nearly six hours of De Niro running time. The two roles, coming so close together, can be seen as twin peaks of his career this decade. There was no doubt that here was a man who could still dominate the screen.

A brief aside before leaving the partnership with Scorsese altogether. When the director was struggling to raise cash for his long-treasured project, **The Last Temptation Of Christ**, De Niro offered to take the lead role if it would attract financial backers. Knowing that this was a gesture born out of friendship rather than a desire to make the film, Scorsese explored other avenues. Fine though Willem Dafoe was in the finished picture, it's tantalising to envisage exchanges between De Niro's Jesus and Harvey Keitel as Judas. That might have made the journey begun in **Mean Streets** complete.

Although De Niro's stature within the industry is such that he has seldom been denied a part he truly desired, there is one famous instance of him missing out. Francis Ford Coppola saw practically every young actor in the country when casting for **The Godfather**, and De Niro was up for the part of Sonny, fiery first born son of Don Vito Corleone. Coppola was impressed by the unknown's screen test, but felt that his intensity was such that he might draw the audience's attention away from the central figure of Michael Corleone, and unbalance the entire picture. As back-handed compliments go, it's one of the best, though God knows how much more intense De Niro could have been than the eventual choice, James Caan[2].

Midnight Run

A WANTED MAN

There is one other omission from this tome which could be seriously questioned. **Midnight Run** seemed an unusual career choice for the actor. A comedy thriller/road movie in which cynical, bad-tempered bounty hunter Jack Walsh escorts dapper "white collar criminal" Jonathan Mardukis across country to stand trial. What elevates the picture above genre convention are the performances by the two leads. As the embezzler, Charles Grodin is dry, measured and understated, the perfect foil for the permanently enraged De Niro. As you'd expect, the actor convincingly conveys the frustration of an ex-cop forced into a hand-to-mouth existence by police corruption, but more surprising is the expert comic timing he displays. De Niro is hilarious, whether – "I got two words for you: Shut the fuck up" – mocking the pompous Feds on his quarry's trail, or contorting his features into a grimace of ever increasing impatience at Mardukis' incessant whining. As one critic said at the time, although this is the kind of performance and film ignored at Awards ceremonies, when the time comes for the De Niro obituary to be written, **Midnight Run** will be remembered.

This book, however, is far from being an obituary. It's not even an appraisal of a career nearing its end. Instead, it's a study of an actor who has never been more in demand. 1998's **Ronin**, though flawed by a predictable script and flagging pace, is significant for including De Niro's first outing as an action hero, complete with shoot-outs and car chases and unwise assignations with duplicitous women. It also saw the actor pocket his largest wage packet to date, some $12 million. Next up came **Analyse This**, a gangster comedy with Billy Crystal which was the first De Niro film ever to take in excess of $100 million dollars at the American box office. As if determined to experience every aspect of film acting before he's through, the actor will next be seen in his first FX-heavy family movie, when he plays – complete with monocle and prosthetically enhanced chin – the evil Fearless Leader in the live action version of 'toon classic **The Adventures Of Rocky & Bullwinkle**. Perhaps most daringly, he'll also risk his entire reputation and standing as an actor by working for the usually clueless Joel Schumacher on **Flawless** – which is the kind of title vindictive movie critics dream about.

A more varied slate is hard to imagine, and it seems apparent that De Niro, though in his mid-fifties – he was born in New York on August 17th, 1943 – shows no sign of lightening his work load. Maybe being the finest actor of this century isn't enough for him, and he fancies a crack at setting the standard for the next.

NOTES

1. See Steven Bach's *Final Cut*, published by Faber.

2. Coppola remembered De Niro well enough to recommend him to Scorsese for **Mean Streets**, and the rest is movie history.

SEQUEL RITES:
'THE GODFATHER PART II'

"Michael, say goodbye."
—Don Vito Corleone (Robert De Niro), **The Godfather Part II**

Robert De Niro's reputation as a film star with all the chameleon ability of a character actor is founded on his work for Martin Scorsese – notably **Taxi Driver** (1976), in which we are privy to his resculpting as mohawked urban avenger, and **Raging Bull** (1980), frequently cited as the apogee of Method for the pounds De Niro donned as Jake La Motta. But just as intriguing a disappearing act is effected in the movie that first brought Robert De Niro to popular attention, Francis Ford Coppola's **The Godfather Part II** (1974). Fitting around **The Godfather** (1972) like a glove, the sequel permitted Coppola to realise his ambition of telling "a story of a father and son at the same age, in parallel action".[1] What this meant for De Niro was the role of the young Vito Andolini Corleone – essayed as an old man in the original by Marlon Brando. With Brando himself absent due to money wrangles, **The Godfather Part II**'s ability to mesh with its predecessor depended largely on De Niro's invocation of the absent star.

At this point in his career, Robert De Niro certainly had his own, emergent screen persona. His leukaemic catcher in baseball weepie **Bang The Drum Slowly** (1973) had earned critical plaudits while adumbrating the impression made in **Mean Streets** (1973) of a player with a feel for blue-collar realism. As Corleone was in many ways the seminal Italian-American crook, **The Godfather Part II** undoubtedly seemed the perfect move in the wake of **Mean Streets**; moreover, as De Niro had been turned down for **The Godfather** just two years before, the gaining of the part was a measure of his recent success. But, called upon to exercise a wooing cool that would both make sense of Brando's paternalistic allure and contrast with the spiritual malaise afflicting Vito's son Michael (Al Pacino), De Niro nevertheless found himself dancing to another's tune. The fact that he was compelled to imitate Brando's husky whisper almost exclusively in Italian (his few lines of English are largely aphoristic and include a version of Brando's famous "I'll make him an offer he can't refuse") only added to the hamstrung aspect of the job.

The irony is of course that, for his pains, De Niro won the 1975 Academy Award for Best Supporting Actor. If anything, the prize further enhanced the strange, haunted quality of his contribution to the film – for, in 1973, Brando too had been cited by the Academy for the very same role. In the event, Brando refused to collect his second Best Actor Oscar in order

to highlight the plight of Native Americans, sending Indian Nations representative Sacheen Littlefeather in his place. (The gesture angered producers Paramount and their parent company Gulf & Western, possibly explaining why funds weren't forthcoming for Brando's return in **Part II**.) Now, however, an actor had come forward to claim a statuette for Corleone – an actor who was on the brink of becoming the most notable exemplar of Stanislavskian Method since Brando himself and one, indeed, who even moved to Sicily as part of the rehearsal process for **Part II**. By filling the space Brando had created on the Academy's stage, De Niro unwittingly made more complete an already uncanny confusion of identities. With the sequel also marking the cinema debut of Method guru Lee Strasberg – under whom both Brando and De Niro had studied in New York's Actor's Studio – it's hard not to see **Part II** as the movie in which the baton of great American screen acting is passed.[2]

De Niro enjoys the minority of the two-hundred-minute running time of **The Godfather Part II**, whatever version is shown: its seven-and-a-quarter hour amalgamation with **The Godfather – Mario Puzo's The Godfather: The Complete Novel For Television** (1977) – may contain extra footage of Vito's early life, but by opting for a strictly chronological approach, simply makes clearer **Part II**'s weighting in favour of actual star Pacino.[3] Yet the ghostliness De Niro brings to the picture is absolutely key. The impact of the film lies entirely in the ripples, oppositions and rhymes made possible firstly by its status as a sequel, and then by the intermingling of two stories separated even at their nearest point by decades. As Coppola commented, "The movie is meant to be like the *Oresteia*, showing how evil reverberates over a period of generations... It's something in the direction, or in the dialogue, or in the mood of each scene. It's like harmony where one note echoes another. As a whole, the first film ought to haunt the second like a spectre."[4] Building on the cross-cutting that distinguishes the last act of the first **Godfather**, Coppola makes of **Part II** an echo chamber that eventually reveals Michael himself to be an empty vessel, drained of all humanity by a perverse sense of loyalty to the past.

The Godfather Part II begins as **The Godfather** ended – with a respectful kiss for the new Godfather, Michael (Pacino), on acceding to his father's throne. Flashing back to Sicily in 1901, the roots of the Corleone empire are found in childhood trauma as nine-year-old Vito Andolini (Oreste Baldini) witnesses the murder of his entire family at the hands of local Mafia chieftain Don Ciccio (Giuseppe Sillato). Despatched to New York for safety, he is renamed after his hometown, Corleone, and quarantined on Ellis Island with smallpox.

In 1958, on Michael Corleone's Lake Tahoe estate, a lavish party is underway to celebrate eldest son Anthony's first communion. Michael himself is preoccupied with business, negotiating a gaming certificate for one of his new hotels from troublesome Senator Al Geary (G.D. Spradlin) and nurturing a new partnership with Jewish crime lord Hyman Roth (Lee Strasberg). When old retainer Frankie Pentangeli (Michael V. Gazzo) begs for permission to settle a score in New York with Roth-affiliated drug-dealers the Rosato brothers, Michael talks him down.

Outside, it's a far more fractured Corleone family that gathers than graced the wedding reception which opened the first film: Connie (Talia Shire) is an absentee mother on the verge of yet another husband, while Fredo (John Cazale), out-of-control wife in tow, seems more weak-willed than ever. Only Michael's marriage to Kay (Diane Keaton) is strong. But later that night, when an assassination attempt is made on the couple, Michael is forced to flee Nevada, leaving Kay and the children virtual prisoners in their own home.

By 1917, Vito (De Niro) is married with a young son, and works as an errand boy in a grocery store in New York's Hell's Kitchen. One day he is sacked to make way for the nephew of the local Black Hand representative, white-suited extortioner Fanucci (Gaston Moschin). When Clemenza (B. Kirby

Jr), a young hood in a neighbouring apartment, asks Vito to hide a bundle of pistols, he does so, even though he understands what it contains. As a reward, Clemenza takes Vito to the home of a local worthy to steal a carpet.

Michael suggests to Hyman Roth in Miami that Pentangeli was responsible for the bid on his life, and asks to set up a hit. Then, visiting Pentangeli in New York, he accuses Roth instead. Pentangeli agrees to forget his differences with the Rosatos to buy Michael time to discover who it is among the Corleone clan that betrayed him. Accordingly, Pentangeli meets with the brothers – who bungle his murder but are careful to state that they are acting on Michael's orders. Michael's loyal *consigliore* Tom Hagen (Robert Duvall) blackmails Senator Geary by implicating him in a brothel murder.

Michael flies to Cuba to finalise the huge, government-backed casino-hotel deal with the ailing Roth. At a birthday party, Roth divides up his empire, naming Michael as his successor; Michael, however, doubts the stability of Cuba's Batista regime and so withholds his $2m. Fredo arrives, only to let slip that he is in league with Roth and Michael's betrayer. That night, Michael arranges for Roth to be killed, but is frustrated by the communists' New Year's Eve take-over. Returning to Nevada, he is further

distressed to discover that Kay has had a miscarriage.

Vito is preoccupied by the pneumonia afflicting baby Fredo. Fanucci, offended at not having received any of the proceeds from the various robberies carried out by Vito's gang, collars the young man – who persuades partners Clemenza and Tessio (John Aprea) to pay just a portion of what Fanucci demands. He offers the gangster $100. Eventually Fanucci accepts, impressed by Vito's nerve. As Fanucci leaves to swagger through the local *festa*, Vito follows him across the rooftops, shooting him dead at his front door. He returns to the doorstep of his own tenement block and embraces his new son, Michael.

The Corleone family's business affairs become subject to a Senate investigation. Pentangeli's lieutenant Willi Cicci (Joe Spinell) names Michael as the head of the Corleone syndicate. Michael seeks solace from his mother (Morgana King), probing her about his father and the importance of being strong for the family.

Vito now dominates Hell's Kitchen. He resolves an accommodation problem for an acquaintance of his wife. At first the landlord bridles at the interference, then caves in on learning Vito's identity. Vito and gang establish Genco Olive Oil Importers as a business front.

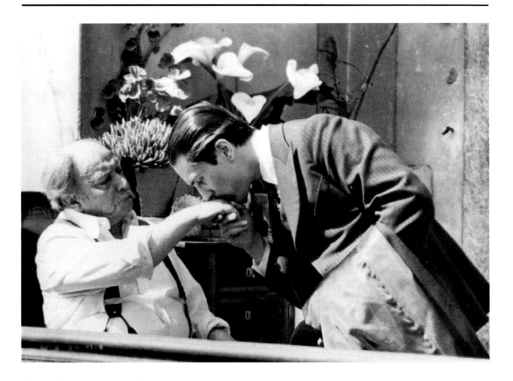

At the Senate hearings, Michael, counselled by Tom Hagen, denies all accusations before reminding the committee of his conspicuous service during World War II. Pentangeli, terrorised by the manufactured attempt on his life, agrees to testify against the Corleones. Michael quizzes Fredo about the plots against him. Fredo explains his act of betrayal by way of the resentment he felt at being passed over in favour of his younger brother. Michael cuts all ties with Fredo.

On the morning Pentangeli is due to give evidence, Michael and Hagen arrive in court with Frankie Pentangeli's Sicilian brother (Salvatore Po). Sight of him is enough to convince the old man to deny all knowledge of the Corleones' Mafia activities. Kay informs Michael that she is leaving him, and that she aborted their last child to prevent bringing another Corleone into the world. Michael assaults her, vowing that she will never have custody of the children.

Vito, wife and family arrive in Sicily on the pretext of visiting Genco's olive oil interests. At the home of the now decrepit Don Ciccio, Vito announces that his father's name was Antonio Andolini, then butchers the *capo*.

Fredo returns to Lake Tahoe for the funeral of Mama Corleone. Connie begs Michael to forgive their brother, pleading for what is left of the family to come together. Michael embraces Fredo, but looks to his lieutenant, Rocco (Tom Rosqui), as he does so.

Insistent that his enemies be removed, Michael persuades an unwilling Hagen to visit Pentangeli in prison. There, Hagen urges Pentangeli to commit suicide so as to ensure the future well being of his family. Pentangeli complies, slitting his wrists in the manner of his Roman forebears. At the same time, Roth is gunned down at Miami airport after being denied entry to Israel. Out on Lake Tahoe, Fredo and Rocco are fishing. As Fredo recites "Hail Marys" to ensure a bigger catch, he too is killed. The shot echoes around the Corleone compound. Visibly aged, Michael stares vacantly, remembering the time he disrupted his father's birthday celebrations by joining the Marines.

Francis Ford Coppola has never quite escaped the influence of sixties mentor Roger Corman, to whom obeisance is paid in **Part II** by having him cameo as an investigating Senator. Even Coppola's most careful film, **The Conversation** (1974 – made directly before **Part II**), could not resist a fog-strewn nightmare that would have been more at home in one of Corman's Poe gothics, while **Apocalypse Now** (1979) benefited hugely from the director's inability to impose himself on the shoot[5]. Throughout the **Godfather** series, Coppola frequently reveals his vulgarian bent through operatic gesture, whether in the grand parallels created by editors Peter Reynolds, Peter Zinner and Barry Malkin, the melodramatic use of Nino Rota's *Love Theme*, the pointlessly over-extended metaphor of Roth serving birthday cake while slicing up his empire – or, indeed, the staging of Mascagni's Sicilian opera *Cavalleria Rusticana* in **The Godfather Part III** (1990). It's typical of Coppola, therefore, that in **Part II** he calls upon regular production designer Dean Tavoularis and **Godfather** cinematographer Gordon Willis to devise a crude visual opposition between father and son. In spite of itself, it works – and again, it's in no small part due to De Niro, who delivers a performance that surreptitiously brings the two worlds in line.

The last American film to be processed using the dye transfer Technicolor system, **The Godfather Part II** portrays Vito's life in the same burnished tones that distinguished **The Godfather** itself; what Willis styles "an almost Kodachromey, 1942 kind of feel"[6]. Sicilian scenes flooded with light, several roguish comic interludes and all the sociable panoply required of a turn-of-the-century immigrant quarter complement this warm, nostalgic palette of New York browns. In its midst, Vito is almost a Robin Hood figure, a clear code of morality driving him both to revenge his family's homicide and to replace that foppish parody of rectitude, Fanucci, with a more responsible alternative: himself. Meanwhile, the wicked Michael inhabits a cold and desultory environment. Far more often placed inside than out, he is usually

found in low-ceilinged rooms with obscured windows, dominated by shadows thrown by an icy pallor. Indeed, so much is he a friend of the dark that at the finale even Fredo's execution takes place in the half-light of dusk. And as for the Lake Tahoe estate on which it occurs – separated by thousands of miles from Manhattan's bustle – it feels the antithesis of the old, healthful, Little Italy community ways. When, in the opening party sequence, Pentangeli, exasperated by the un-Italian glitz, demands a tarantella, the orchestra mocks him with "Pop Goes the Weasel" instead.[7]

On the surface at least, De Niro is every inch the attractive, ingratiating gangster the idealised depiction of his rise to power would have him be. Memorably described by one critic as "a limpid-eyed Bronzino"[8], his Vito Corleone – a moody, strikingly handsome man of action – flags the actor up as romantic lead material, and is surely the inspiration for British pop group Bananarama's later paean, "Robert De Niro's Waiting (Talking Italian)". Notwithstanding, the actor uses Vito's machismo to hint at personality defects that connect tantalisingly with Michael's own terrible deadness of spirit. As a boy, Vito is shown as something of an observer, witnessing his mother's death and, later, gazing out impassively over New York. When De Niro assumes the part, he expands on that becalmed gaze to such an extent that we are thrown into doubt as to the thoughts behind those eyes. Our suspicions culminate in the eerie moment of stillness – towel aflame around a smoking pistol – that follows Fanucci's murder, but a chill can also be felt in such earlier scenes as when Vito spies on Fanucci abusing a friend's girl. This cauterised sensibility even puts question marks over Vito's home life. At once spectacularly loving and so spectacularly uncommunicative that Mama Corleone appears to exist solely to make babies and spaghetti, Vito in De Niro's grasp seems, in crucial moments, a dubious head for a family empire.

De Niro's performance also justifies some of the larger ambitions entertained for the **Godfather** series. His disconcerting tendency for feigned bonhomie – nowhere better seen than in the glib fealty exhibited toward Don Ciccio directly before his slaughter – manages, for instance, to intimate a culture in which deference to family (with all the good behaviour that that implies) leads with horrible inexorability to violence and revenge. And De Niro's conveyance of this as a peculiarly Italian, Catholic trait doesn't stop at his Latinate good looks, either. For here the actor's distinctive taciturnity cleverly becomes part and parcel of the Sicilian code of omertà, "silence" – something later deployed in the Senate courtroom to keep Pentangeli from turning state's evidence. (Coppola may be a family man to the extent of employing his father to conduct Rota's score and his cousin to play Connie, but the two 1970s **Godfather** films make as violently ambivalent a statement about the strengths of Catholicism as does colleague William Friedkin's contemporaneous hit, **The Exorcist**.)

Most importantly perhaps, the links De Niro forges between young Vito and the vitiated Corleone clan of the 1950s lend credence to the notion that the **Godfather** saga operates as a critique of America itself. Coppola concurred with Brando that the Mafia was a metaphor for the United States. As the director said in 1972: "Both the Mafia and America have roots in Europe. [B]oth the Mafia and America feel they are benevolent organisations. Both the Mafia and America have their hands stained with blood from what it is necessary to do to preserve their interests. Both are totally capitalistic phenomena and basically have a profit motive."[9] But, as Coppola went on to identify, the appeal of the first film lay in the extent to which its gangsters differed from the government machine: "When the court fails you and the whole state system fails you, you can go to the old man – Don Corleone – and say, 'Look what they did to me', and you get justice."[10] The epic sense of corruption De Niro introduces into **The Godfather Part II** counters this romantic notion, helping to shift the balance so that now the Corleones function as a simulacrum for the American State.

Assisted by a budget of $13m (more than twice that of the original **Godfather**), Coppola works hard to freight **Part II** with historical and political resonance. As well as drawing parallels between G.D. Spradlin's racist Senator and the clannish bigotry of the Mafia, he utilises a Statue-of-Liberty motif to suggest Vito's rise to power is the American Dream made flesh and includes veiled references to an array of Presidential duplicity. The syndicate support for Batista's Cuban regime is pre-eminent in this respect, but, in addition, Michael's Lake Tahoe estate recalls the Kennedys' Massachusetts compound, Roth's assassination imitates that of Lee Harvey Oswald, and the senate investigations ape the Watergate hearings (high in the popular consciousness in 1974). When, at the end of the movie, we are reminded that Michael was once a soldier, it becomes obvious that in his developing character we have been presented with the two faces of modern USA. The one socially responsible, with a sense of America as consisting of its citizenry, and the other venal and paranoid, with the country viewed merely as an opportunity for gain.

The Godfather Part II is by no stretch of the imagination a flawless film. The rhyming structure results in moments of wilful obscurantism: to illustrate Michael's loosening grip, the bungled assassinations of Pentangeli and Roth are designed to mimic the efficient dispatches of the first movie, but the effect, especially in the case of Pentangeli, is to muffle the plot. And, as even Coppola has noted[11], Pacino essays Michael with a wearisomely one-note sense of corruption.[12]

What finally makes **The Godfather Part II** great, however – indeed, the only sequel to win the Best Picture Oscar to date – is the conflation of De Niro's gaze with the black-eyed stare of Pacino. Critics of the initial instalment accused it of being an immoral apology for America's ethnic gangsters. Though neither the Mafia nor the Cosa Nostra were actually mentioned until **Part II** (sensitivities dictated that the phrase "the five families" be used instead), it's undeniably the case that **The Godfather** did induce a pop cultural obsession with Italian syndicate crime. In many ways of course, **Part II** increased the fascination. But what it also contrived, by establishing an equality between the fresh-faced Vito and his power-addled son, was a deglamorisation of the original picture, so deepening and broadening the whole. That De Niro brought this about by improving on Brando surely places **The Godfather Part II** among his most significant achievements.

NOTES

1. "The Godfather Part II: A Look Back", **The Godfather Part II 25th Anniversary Edition**, Paramount, 1997.

2. Pacino was, admittedly, another notable Actor's Studio alumnus of the time, but one whose major triumphs were on stage. On Lee Strasberg's death in 1982, Pacino, with Ellen Burstyn, became co-artistic director of the Actor's Studio for two years.

3. Coppola biographer Peter Cowie estimates Vito's story takes up a quarter of the film's running time. Peter Cowie, *Coppola*, London: Faber & Faber, rev. ed. 1998, p.114.

4. Ibid., p.101.

5. Detailed in Fax Bahr and George Hickenlooper's documentary **Hearts Of Darkness: A Filmmaker's Apocalypse** (1991). As Coppola states at the 1979 Cannes press conference with which it opens: "My film is not a movie. My film is not about Vietnam. It *is* Vietnam. It's what it was really like. It was crazy... We were in the jungle. We had access to too much money, too much equipment, and little by little we went insane."

6. Cowie, p.81.

7. Considering Pentangeli's later betrayal of Michael, the choice of tune is ever so slightly sinister.

8. Carlos Clarens, "The Godfather Saga", *Film Comment*, January/February 1978, p.22.

9. Stephen Farber, "Coppola And The Godfather", *Sight & Sound*, Autumn 1972, p.223.

10. Ibid., p.223.

11. "He's the same man from beginning to end... very rarely having a big climactic scene where an actor can unload, like blowing the spittle out of the tube of a trombone." Cowie, p.100.

12. Later in their careers, both De Niro and Pacino would play the Devil, but despite Pacino's bandstanding in **The Devil's Advocate** (1997), De Niro brings more fun and variety to a much slimmer part in **Angel Heart** (1987).

'1900'

It is one of those stories of a "brave" auteur facing up to philistine Hollywood executives, in an attempt to protect his vision, his integrity and his sanity. Think of D. W. Griffith's **Intolerance**, Orson Welles' **Magnificent Ambersons**, Visconti's **The Leopard**, Francis Ford Coppola's **One From The Heart**, or Michael Cimino's **Heaven's Gate**. Think of Bernardo Bertolucci's **1900** (**Novecento**, 1976) in that company. And, inevitably, think of the phrase "flawed masterpiece".

It was unlikely that it was ever going to be anything else. Bertolucci was hot property after the critical and commercial success of **Last Tango In Paris**, so he found it easy to raise the $8 million the film was rumoured to have cost in a complicated deal involving Paramount, 20th Century Fox and United Artists. At the time, it was undoubtedly the most expensive film ever made in Italy. The director would be given free rein to make a film that was extremely personal and explicitly political, while incorporating Hollywood's grand production values. After a turbulent filming in the North Italian province of Emelia (the usual: escalating budget, constant rewrites, and **Last Tango** star Maria Schneider, an actress in a key role, walking out of the film – and, seemingly, out of the film industry), the film was submitted as a five and a half hour epic to be released in two parts. This was the version that was released in Europe, but Paramount, who owned the rights to its American release, balked at its length and insisted that the film be cut to the three hours and fifteen minutes stipulated in their contract. Bertolucci edited the film down to four and a half hours. Still not happy, Paramount set about cutting the film themselves, much to Bertolucci's chagrin. Whether or not a three hour fifteen minute version exists, it was never screened for the public. The film was released in the United States and Britain in its four and a half hour, English language version over a year after its European release, to mixed reviews and mediocre box office. A curious postscript to all this was that, unlike other directors who have been put into such compromising positions, who may confront the studio or insist their names are taken off the credits, Bertolucci seems to have been a willing accomplice in his own compromises, to the extent that he has said that he felt "completely free" to make his own cuts and welcomed the chance to "better" his film with the English language version[1]. Which is not what he was saying in his tirades to the press while Paramount were withholding his film. Either he genuinely had a change of heart, or the compromises went further than the cuts he made to his film.

Given these circumstances, it is amazing the film exists at all, never mind that two versions of it exist. Here lies perhaps the biggest problem with the film. During filming, the actors spoke in their own language, and they

would re-dub their voices for the print that would be shown in their homelands. Here was a film with an American and a Frenchman in its lead roles, surrounded by actors from Canada, Italy and Germany. The Italian version is obviously regarded as the "original", and while this is clearly a misnomer, it does highlight the unsatisfying sound of the film. Dubbing is still a practice used widely in Europe, but regarded with some disdain in Britain and America. It is certainly disconcerting watching actors of the stature of Burt Lancaster or Sterling Hayden and seeing their lips move totally out of sync with what you are hearing. At the same time, for a film that goes to such length to recreate its period, and that strives to be realistic, hearing the Italian ruling classes of the early twentieth century speak in, as one critic described De Niro's accent, a "Lower East Side variant of Italo-American"[2], it is no less off-putting.

De Niro plays Alfredo Berlinghieri, born, in 1900, into a wealthy family, inheritor of "his father's eyes... and his grandfather's money". His story is interlinked with that of Olmo Dalco (Gerard Depardieu), an illegitimate peasant, who is born on the same day, just minutes earlier, "another mouth to feed, another bottom to wipe". As they grow up closely together, a mutual respect and fondness develop, despite their class differences. After

World War One, Olmo comes back from the fighting to work the land with his people, and encourages resistance to the oppressive aristocracy. Alfredo escapes from playing soldier in his loft to discover the playboy lifestyle (including the pleasures of sex and cocaine) under the guidance of his flamboyant uncle. Bought back to his home after the death of his father, he marries the free-spirited Ada (Dominique Sanda), and struggles with his new responsibilities. As Italy succumbs to fascism, represented by Donald Sutherland's ambitious, blackshirted foreman, Attilla, Alfredo's liberalism proves ineffectual. At death of Mussolini, Communism is embraced by the peasants, Alfredo is put on trial and found guilty by the Emilian peasants. His sentence is never set, as this proves to be a false dawn, and Olmo and Alfredo squabble pitifully into their old age.

De Niro's voice is not the only thing here that stands out as different from his other performances. It appears to be the only time in his career that he has played an absolute weakling: men with weaknesses, weak men with hidden depths of strength or knowledge, but never one as passive as Alfredo Berlinghieri.

As the critic Richard Corliss wrote: "from childhood to middle age, he does nothing, thinks little, feels hardly at all"[3]. He is spoilt by his family, and seems incapable of confronting either the peasants or the fascists. When his wife leaves him, is accepting and barely surprised. He is impotent in every sense of the word.

Elevating his collaborations with Scorsese, critic Ian Penman dismisses De Niro's performances for other directors. He claims that in "epic sweeps [such as **1900**], he is little more than an empty centre of gravity, a mere glint[of the presence, the method"[4]. De Niro himself was apparently none too happy with his performance. One of the reasons he took the role was because he shared an enthusiasm for improvisation with Bertolucci. He had visited the Emelia valley at his own expense months before shooting began, preparing for the role and "becoming" Alfredo. However, he found Bertolucci less collaborative and more dictatorial than he had expected, the director frustrating the actor with his frequent rewrites, and actually instructing him on how to deliver his lines. "Alfredo was such an observer," said De Niro, "that it was difficult to fill him in."[5] This view was developed by Pauline Kael, who chastised Bertolucci in her review of the of the film: "He has cast De Niro, an actor whose responsiveness to the camera derives from his reserves of passion, and having cast this man, has not allowed him any passion. Bertolucci, locking himself away, has locked De Niro out as an actor – gutted him. His Alfredo is an unfinished man: a man who hasn't tested himself. He's too emasculated even to suffer. Alfredo is the pampered, bourgeois liberal that Bertolucci guiltily fears himself to be"[6].

It would be unwise, though, to dismiss the film, which has so much to recommend it, as merely a blip in De Niro's early career. Extravagant and ambitious, the genuine International nature of the project would have made it a fascinating experiment, if nothing else, but it is also a visual feast, finding beauty not only in the magnificent Italian countryside but in the interiors, the homes of peasants and aristocrats alike. There is no doubt that Bertolucci recognised and harnessed De Niro's iconic presence (as well as Depardieu's), in the same way Scorsese and Coppola had before him, but this was still before Travis Bickle or Jake La Motta, and the director deserves some praise for that.

Bertolucci has never been a director to shy away from sexual themes in his films, so much so that he appears to have latterly gained a reputation as the "dirty old man" of cinema. The attitude he adopts to sex in **1900** seems curiously ambivalent. The rather lazy connection between sex and death is exposed in a bizarre scene involving Attila, his Lady Macbeth-like mistress, Regina (Laura Betti), and a child who they sexually abuse and eventually kill by dashing its brains out against a stone wall, maniacally laughing at their own brutality. They later try and pin the murder on Olmo,

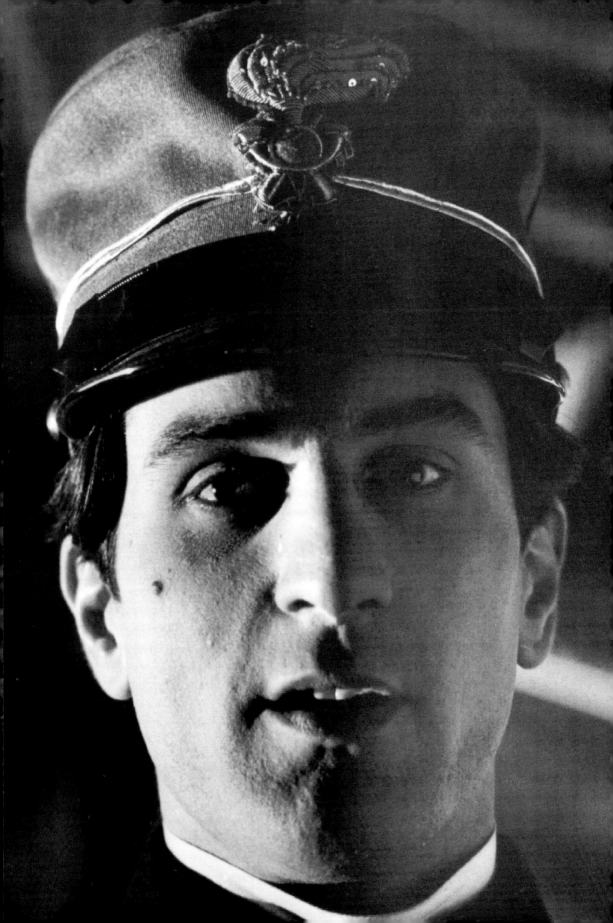

and Attilla and his Nazi chums give him a beating, as Alfredo looks helplessly on. Is this an illustration of fascist evil or sexual immaturity? The relationship between Olmo and Alfredo has overtones of homosexuality that are never truly developed, but which are presented as being perfectly natural and unselfconscious. On his return from the war, Olmo greets Alfredo and they grapple playfully in the same place they compared penises as children, Alfredo declaring Olmo "my hero". At one point the two men actually end up naked in bed together, albeit joined by an epileptic prostitute. Throughout the film, there are suggestions of Alfredo's homosexuality. After failing to satisfy Regina, Alfredo's cousin, she declares that she needs a "real man" instead of Alfredo and turns to Attilla. He is drawn to his homosexual uncle. A lack of sex is one of the reasons his marriage breaks down. It is in these scenes that De Niro seems ideal for the role. Not only is he capable of conveying his passivity, but with his floppy fringe, his perfect skin, the white suit he wears to his father's funeral, he has rarely looked more camp, or for that matter, more beautiful on screen. Acting against the gallic rusticity of Depardieu, the contrast is precious. This actor, famed for playing gangsters, vigilantes and hard men, has never looked so gay. The theme of aristocratic impotence is extended to patriarch Burt Lancaster (another star once famed for his athletic virility), who hangs himself in the stables after failing to achieve erection at the hands of a milk maid.

Some Paramount executives called **1900** "a little too red"[7] for their tastes before they finally released it, and while the film is undoubtedly left wing, its politics are too confused to pin an ideology to it. Our sympathies are always with the peasants and their resistance, but there is a refusal to romanticise or be idealistic about their situation. These are people who are socialist "right down to the holes in their pockets" (Alfredo later repeats this line, naively, in an attempt to impress Olmo). This is the area Bertolucci grew up in, a place "that has been communist since communism has existed"[8], yet there is no trace of the sentimentality you may expect in such a film. Only the eternal summer of the childhood scenes are a possible concession to this, but these are aesthetic as much as political concessions, and one might make comparisons here to, say, John Boorman's **Hope And Glory**, or Zeffirelli's **Tea With Mussolini** to see how far Bertolucci has gone to avoid nostalgia. It is the middle classes that Bertolucci has his real knives out for. They are the ambitious, demonic Nazis, Attilla and Regina, used by the landowners and the church, who "don't want violence or vengeance, we just want order", and who become murderers of the working class. There is some sympathy with the aristocrats, who, despite their weaknesses, are never evil, and seem to regard the fascists with distaste for their crudity, rather than their political views. Alfredo and his grandfather particularly try and empathise with the

peasants and respect the dignity of labour, but they accept their birthright and can never truly understand or fully ingratiate themselves to their workers. Of course, the noble peasants who are the heroes, particularly Olmo, who seems almost too good to be true. He is a caring, considerate man, worshipped by his fellow peasants, virile and physical, who has no fear when confronted by Attilla or the King's troops. Again, the contrast with De Niro's Alfredo is a pointed one. Depardieu's Olmo, active and virtuous, is everything he is not.

Bertolucci's intention was to make a popular political film about the class struggle that would appeal to a mass audience, and this may explain his lack of subtlety. De Niro himself declared the process "a new way to make political film", adding "in practically all my films there has been a political focus in some form or other, however detached. But now, the attitude towards politics in the cinema has changed. During the Sixties, one thought political cinema could have an effect. I now believe that was an illusion"[9]. The failing of the film's polemic lies in its ambiguous ending. The peasants accuse a broken Alfredo of being a parasite and an exploiter. His defence is that he never meant any harm. Olmo argues that his friend is guilty, but that it does not matter any more, because they are all equal. He wants the landowner dead, but only symbolically. As the other peasants bray for blood, a peace-keeping force arrives to confiscate their weapons. The peasants disperse, and Alfredo hisses that "the padrone is still alive". He starts to squabble with Alfredo in the empty courtyard, and then the scene cuts to the pair as old men, comically wrestling each other, a continuation of the class struggle. Then Alfredo lies down in front of a train, something they did as children for dares, but now as a suicide. Bertolucci declares that he does this in acceptance of "the validity of the proletariat's ideas"[10], but why draw this out? If Bertolucci conformed to Marxist theory, why is the possibility of change dismissed? And why, as the old men paw and slap each other, is the suggestion that the struggle we have witnessed is utterly pointless, that things are just going to continue as they are until death? Maybe ending the film with the death of Attila would have been even more simplistic and even less subtle, and a wholehearted victory for the peasants untrue to history (Italy was about to be governed by a Christian Democrat coalition). Still, you get the feeling that Bertolucci's own position as bourgeois communist informs this conclusion; committed to the cause, but unable to wholeheartedly endorse it for fear of losing his own privileged position.

Reflecting on the film in 1991 Bertolucci said, "I wanted to do a movie with a political meaning and dramatic energy that would be seen by a large audience. Maybe I became a little idealistic about it. In **1900**, I wanted to conjugate a very strong political message with Hollywood storytelling. In other words, I wanted to marry socialist realism to **Gone With The Wind**. I think of it as my impossible film"[11].

De Niro was essential to the director's vision in representing Hollywood and Rhett Butler's glamour. To that extent, the actor should be praised for his achievements. Yet the film remains a curiosity in his career, portraying a pathetic character in an expressly political film. He would arguably never do "weak" or "political" again. The same might be said for Bertolucci. Consider the first part of the following quote as true for De Niro as well as his director: "Bertolucci is in no way diminished by **1900**," wrote the critic Leonard Quart at the time of its release. "He is still one of the most exciting young filmmakers around, a director of vaunting ambition and imagination whose capacity growth has no ceiling. One of these years he'll make a Marxist film that will strike the right dialectical balance between Freudian leftism and visual genius."[12] He has never made that film, despite the Oscar glory and career renaissance of **The Last Emperor** over ten years later. However, if **1900** proved "impossible" for Bertolucci, it is still better to applaud an ambitious failure than a safe bet.

NOTES

1. Burgoyne, Robert. *Bertolucci's 1900: A Narrative And Historical Analysis*, Wayne State University Press, 1991.

2. Knight, Arthur. *Saturday Review*.

3. Brode, Douglas. *The Films Of Robert De Niro*, Citadel Press, 1993.

4. Penman, Ian. *Vital Signs*, Serpent's Tail, 1998.

5. Brode, Douglas. *The Films Of Robert De Niro*, Citadel Press, 1993.

6. Kael, Pauline. *For Keeps*, Dutton.

7. Fox, James. "Italy And Fascism: Is It Too Red?", *Sunday Times*, 5 September 1976.

8. Cameron Wilson, James. *The Cinema Of Robert De Niro*, 1986.

9. Cameron Wilson, James. *The Cinema Of Robert De Niro*, 1986.

10. Burgoyne, Robert. *Bertolucci's 1900: A Narrative And Historical Analysis*, Wayne State University Press, 1991.

11. Brode, Douglas. *The Films Of Robert De Niro*, Citadel Press, 1993.

12. Quart, Leonard. "1900: Bertolucci's Marxist Opera", *Cineaste USA* vol. 8, no. 3, 1978.

URBAN NEUROSIS AND DEMENTIA SUBURBIA: 'TAXI DRIVER', TRAVIS BICKLE AND JOHN W HINCKLEY JR

Notoriously, Martin Scorsese's 1976 film **Taxi Driver** – the most praised and damned movie of the 1970s – is believed to have triggered the "copycat" political assassination attempt by John W. Hinckley Jr. on President Ronald Reagan in 1981, illuminating Hinckley's dangerous fixation on actress Jodie Foster, and resulting in the assassin's famous media-hero status. A close examination of both the film and the Hinckley case, however, reveals that Hinckley's obsession with **Taxi Driver** focuses less intensely on the relatively minor role played by Jodie Foster in the movie than on Robert De Niro's tormented portrayal of the unbalanced Travis Bickle. Hinckley's fascination with Bickle's violent urban neurosis leads to the gradual development of his own psychological illness, which several reporters at the trial were led to dub dementia suburbia[1].

TAXI DRIVER: URBAN NEUROSIS

Taxi Driver, like other neo-noir films by Scorsese and his fellow *nouvelle vague*-influenced Hollywood renaissance filmmakers, juxtaposes generic hybridization with allusions to high art and literature. It combines elements of film noir, the Western, the horror film and the urban melodrama in its gritty, disturbing tale of social alienation. Screenwriter Paul Schrader has explicitly described the film as "an attempt to take the European existential hero – that is, the man from *The Stranger*, *Notes From The Underground*, *Nausea*, *Pickpocket*, *Le Fou Follet* and *A Man Escaped* – and set him in an American context"[2]. Other clear influences are John Cassavetes's documentary realism, the metacinematic fantasies of Federico Fellini, Powell and Pressburger's Technicolor expressionism, and the fifties B-movies of "psychotic action and suicidal impulse"[3].

"ALL THE ANIMALS COME OUT AT NIGHT..."

The setting of **Taxi Driver** is the apocalyptic "city of dreadful night" informed by the political paranoia, economic deprivation, inner-city decay, racism and violence of the seventies. This is a New York bristling with alienation, claustrophobia, disillusionment, and the threat of urban violence: an

allegorical underworld vision of hell. The streets are either slick and rainy or oppressively hot, filled with open sewers and manhole covers from which steam vapours rise in cloudy gusts. Red neon lights illuminate the faces of lost souls, the drifters and prostitutes whom De Niro transports from place to place, wandering hypnotically through seedy streets and theatre marquees advertising horror and porno movies[4]. Bickle is disgusted by this world of sleaziness and urban decay:

"All the animals come out at night – whores, skunk pussies, buggers, queers, fairies, dopers, junkies, sick, venal. Some day a real rain will come and wash all this scum off the streets... This city here is like an open sewer, you know. It's full of filth and scum. And sometimes I can hardly take it... Sometimes I go out and smell it, I get headaches, it's so bad, you know..."

This hellish vision of bars and porn theatres is a vivid kaleidoscope of colour and movement, "vibrantly alive with the iridescence of corruption"[5]. Its inhabitants are johns and hookers, clients and cabbies, an anonymous black glanced walking down the street muttering "I'll kill 'em", a shopkeeper smiling amiably one moment, and the next savagely mutilating a corpse with an iron bar. This is a landscape whose apocalyptic decadence impels Bickle's gradual descent into a very specific kind of insanity: urban psychosis, the madness of the city.

"DAYS GO ON AND ON. THEY DON'T END..."

The hallmark of this fascinating film is the tremendous ability of Robert De Niro to totally immerse himself in the character of Travis Bickle, an enigmatic loner twitching with psychotic energy and violent tensions. Bickle has been described as a man "with a vague resemblance to nearly every misanthrope, mass-murderer, plane hi-jacker, or political assassin of the past two decades, and with a vague resemblance, also, to every man's next door neighbour"[6]. Douglas Brode describes him as "a remarkably unique human being, yet also an effectively universal symbol for the walking wounded who have, since the culture shocks of the late sixties, inhabited the mean streets of our major metropolises (along with our movie screens) in ever-increasing numbers"[7]. Some twenty-five years later, Travis Bickle still remains the single character with whom De Niro is most often associated, a character of whom he has spoken off-screen with uncharacteristic eloquence. Claims De Niro:

"I got this image of Travis as a crab. I just had that image of him... You know how a crab sort of walks sideways and has a gawky, awkward movement? Crabs are very straightforward, but straightforward to them is going to the left and to the right. They turn sideways, that's the way they're built."[8]

Previously considered for the role of Travis Bickle were Robert Blake, Jeff Bridges, and farcically, Neil Diamond, none of whom could have brought to the part the kind of precision, texture, depth and edginess of De Niro's portrayal. The critics all agreed. *Variety* insisted that De Niro gives the role the precise blend of awkwardness, naivete, and latent violence which makes Travis a character who is "compelling even when he is at his most revolting". Arthur Knight, writing in the *Hollywood Reporter*, argued that De Niro "manages to make a repulsive creature constantly credible and sometimes sympathetic". Pauline Kael, writing in the *New Yorker*, observed that "Robert De Niro is in almost every frame; thin faced, as handsome as Robert Taylor one moment and cagey, ferrety, like Cagney the next...". And, according to Jack Kroll in *Newsweek*:

"First and last, **Taxi Driver** belongs to Robert De Niro, the most remarkable young actor of the American screen. What the film comes down to is a grotesque *pas de deux* between Travis and the City, and De Niro has the dance quality that most great film actors have had, whether it's *allegro* like Cagney, or *largo* like Brando. De Niro controls his body like a moving sculpture. Once, seething with frustration, he takes a swig from a beer can and his head snaps into a quick, complex spasm of thwarted rage. Trying to ingratiate himself with a Secret Service man, his entire conversation comes out of a tilted-up, twisty-smiling face that's a diagram of social unease. By the time he's through, De Niro has created a total behavioral system for [Travis], which has a macabre comedy."[9]

The shuffling De Niro is plagued by a litany of attributes and characteristics which, along with his nervous demeanour and dishevelled appearance, lead to identify him as what David Weaver has described as "a recognizable 'modern' (rather than mythic) type: the urban neurotic"[10].

The first of these attributes is strong evidence of post-traumatic stress disorder. Bickle offers only a few biographical facts about his background, but we do learn that he's a twenty-six year old ex-marine, possibly a battle-scarred Vietnam vet. His marine battle jacket has "King Kong Brigade" patches on it, and his psychological profile approximates those of war-zone combatants. He tells his boss at the cab company that he was discharged in May 1973, and his exact whereabouts and activities in the intervening three years are left unexplained. He seems to be a compulsive wanderer, perpetually anxious and unable to rest, and takes the job as a taxi driver because of his chronic insomnia, having previously spent his nights wandering the streets. "I can't sleep nights," he complains, in a nervous voice, and can find nothing meaningful to do during the days. His boss suggests he try hanging out in porno theatres:

Bickle: I know. I tried that.
Boss: So whaddya do now?
Bickle: I ride around nights mostly. Subways, buses. Figure, you know, I'm gonna do that, I might as well get paid for it.

He also manifests signs of acute hypochondria, complaining about headaches brought on by the smells of the city and of the dead flowers in his apartment, rejected offerings of love. Later on, in the flat interior monologue that accompanies him through the city, he speculates that he might have stomach cancer. "I shouldn't complain, though," he adds. "You're only as healthy, you're only as healthy as you feel. You're only... as... healthy... as... you... feel".

The twitching De Niro's urban neurosis seems to revolve around a crisis of repressed sexuality. Back inside the cab company's garage in his stall at the end of his shift (six to six), he narrates with self-loathing how he has to clean the interior of his cab after each shift. "Each night, when I return the cab to the garage," he intones, sardonically, "I have to clean the come off the back seat. Some nights, I clean off the blood". His status as a silent player in the perverse games of sexual commerce that nightly surround him serves only to stockpile more ammunition in his own arsenal of repressed sexuality. Alone during the early morning hours, he walks through the red light district and spends his free time in a Triple-X porno theatre, deliberately participating in the same scenes of degradation that he seems to find so repellent by night. Tormented by a turbulent sexual anxiety that he seems unable to acknowledge, even to himself, these violent impulses eventually begin to rupture the neurotic Bickle's own sense of identity. He starts popping pills to keep calm.

"I THINK YOU'RE A LONELY PERSON..."

What makes things worse is Bickle's complete isolation and growing sense of alienation from others. De Niro plays Travis as a complete loner, endlessly striving to bring to an end his crisis of identity, to give meaning to an otherwise insignificant life[11]. Isolated not just from other people but from the society in which he lives, Bickle's inability to connect seems to be expressive of a more general state of the psychological or even epistemological alienation of the modern subject. His predicament seems to suggest that "the fundamental human condition is one of estrangement, both from other people and from all systems of order, with the result that the onus is placed on the individual to produce meaning in a world which is insensible to his or her existence in it"[12].

Incapable of accepting his estrangement from others as the essential human condition, Bickle begins to regard the people outside his taxicab as specifically threatening to him. De Niro's memorably droning voiceover records Travis's cynical thoughts from the tattered journal he keeps in a school composition book purchased at a dime store. His main predicament is the fact that his life seems empty and meaningless, which leads him to spend longer and longer hours with the "scum" he's grown to hate:

"May 10th. Thank god for the rain which has helped wash away the garbage and trash off the sidewalks. I'm working long hours now, six in the afternoon to six in the morning. Sometimes even eight in the morning, six days a week. Sometimes seven days a week. It's a long hustle but it keeps me real busy. I can take in three, three fifty a week. Sometimes even more when I do it off the meter..."

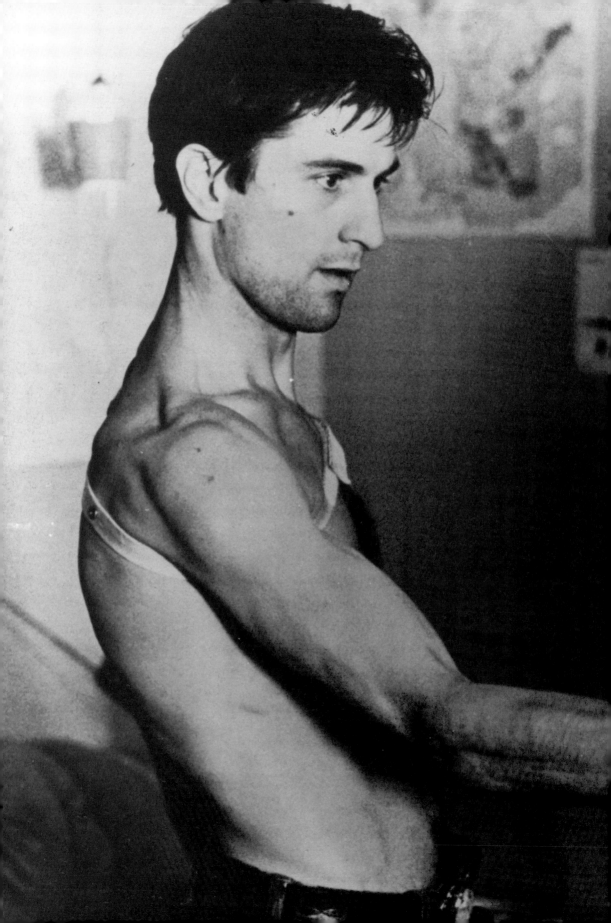

"A WALKING CONTRADICTION"

De Niro's virtuoso performance fills Travis Bickle with little tics and nervous twitches, the helpless death spasms of a contradictory creature trapped between the world of the day and the world of the night. He reminds Betsy of the lyrics of a song by Kris Kristofferson – "he's a prophet and a pusher, partly truth and partly fiction, a walking contradiction". It seems symptomatic of Bickle's ambiguous position in his society – embodied by De Niro's edgy, restless physical demeanour – that he's suspected by pimps and prostitutes of being a cop or a narc, and by secret service agents of being a political assassin. Similarly, he violently insists on his contempt for the night people, the pimps and pushers, yet converses more easily with them than with day-people like Betsy, just as he chooses to work at night, escaping the daylight into the artificial night of porno theatres.[13]

This sense of contradiction is carried over into the way De Niro conveys Bickle's sense of unease about his own body, and his sense of anxiety about the tensions it contains. Feelings of bodily fragmentation – another symptom of urban neurosis – are also evoked by the film's image-track, which is full of shots of Travis's eyes in the taxi rear-view mirror, shots of the back of the head, headless torsos, torsoless heads, close-ups of arms and heads, and various overhead shots of tables, counters and desks with hands extending over them. The voiceover extracts from Bickle's diary, read in De Niro's deadpan voice, also bespeak psychic fragmentation in the form of a disembodied voice laying bare his soul to an unseen listener. Richard Martin explains how we always see the New York environment from Bickle's psychologically unstable perspective:

"[A]ll that is contained in the frame becomes on extension of Travis's troubled psyche, hence the visual stylization (the use of slow-motion and jump-cut editing, the expressionism of the colours), and the one-dimensionality of many of the characters who are little more than ciphers for aspects of Travis's own personality... In fact, Scorsese's modernization of noir expressionism, his stylistic experimentation, and his occasional employment of state-of-the-art technology frequently encourage the reader to identify with the neuroses, obsessions, and paranoia of his troubled protagonists as they negotiate the characters' complex psychic geographies."[14]

These images of fragmentation serve to foreground the film's most notorious sequence, in which an increasingly unbalanced De Niro glares at himself angrily in the mirror and recites conversations in which he threatens and insistently challenges his own image in the guise of an imaginary enemy:

"Huh? Huh? I'm faster than you, you fucking son of a bitch. I saw you coming. Fuck. Shit-heel. I'm standing here. You make the move. You make the move. It's your move. Don't try it, you fucker. You talking to me? You talking to me? You talking to me? Well, who the hell else are you talking to? You talking to me? Well, I'm the only one here. Who the fuck do you think you're talking to? Oh yeah?"

Bickle's psychic fragmentation leads him to pose compulsively in front of the mirror, but always in order to reinforce his neurotic fantasies, never to question them, never to "look at his own eyeballs". ("What makes you so high and mighty?" the aptly-named Iris asks him at one point. "Didn't you ever try looking at your own eyeballs in the mirror?".) Yet Bickle seems almost as incapable of recognizing his literal reflection in the mirror as he is of recognizing his moral and psychological reflection in the character of Iris's pimp, Sport (Harvey Keitel)[15]. It seems ironic that this collapse of identity should be the result of Bickle's tormented, agonized obsession with his own sense of self – what he describes as "morbid self-attention".

Although his communications with others are halting and inarticulate, Bickle's journal records a tortured, skewered, eloquent record of the utter monotony of his existence:

"Loneliness has followed me my whole life. Everywhere. In bars, in cars, sidewalks, stores, everywhere. There's no escape. I'm god's lonely man. June 8th... The days can go on with regularity over and over, one day indistinguishable from the next. A long continuous chain."

Just as Bickle's failure in human interaction sees him reduced to communicating with himself through his diary and his mirror, so his sexual and vocational failures lead him to lie to his parents about the kind of life he leads in New York. He sends them a card in which he claims that he is unable to give out his address because "the sensitive nature of my work for the government demands utmost secrecy. I know you will understand. I am healthy and well and making lots of money". He also tells them that he's been "going with a girl for several months and I know you would be proud if you could see her. Her name is Betsy but I can tell you no more than that".

Eventually, inevitably, the psychic fragmentation becomes apocalyptic. Unable to interact with the people who surround him, and disconnected from the place he inhabits, De Niro's journey through the violent streets of New York City becomes a journey into the depths of his own troubled psyche, an impossible quest for spiritual purity and integrated identity[16]. At first, he goes to fellow driver Wizard (Peter Boyle) and tries inarticulately to explain his deteriorating mental condition, claiming that he's starting to get "bad ideas"

in his head. Wizard tells him to "go out and get laid, get drunk, you know, do anything", because "we're all fucked, more or less, you know". De Niro is not comforted, and as his urban neurosis begins to build, there is almost an entropic trajectory toward solitude, alienation and silence[17]. His sense of isolation is neatly encapsulated in the café scene with his taxi driving colleagues, in which he is completely isolated in his own frame, or physically fragmented in the framing of others[18]. In the same scene, the anxiety-ridden De Niro dumps an Alka Seltzer tablet into a glass of water and the camera zooms in and lingers on the fizzing, exploding action. This is clearly symbolic of a precipitous descent into the effervescent disturbances of Travis's inner world, symbolic of a man whose psyche is gradually fragmenting to such an extent that before long, he is able to communicate his response to the urban environment only through violence[19].

"CLOSE TO THE END..."

Bickle's tenuously maintained psychosexual balance is abruptly and violently

disturbed – and the action of the film set in motion – by a crisis which constitutes an enactment of his own repressed sexual desires. Betsy's angry refusal to see him again after he takes her to a pornographic movie leaves De Niro soured and bitter. "You're in hell, and you're gonna die in hell like the rest of them," he shouts at Betsy, whom he once thought of as an "angel". The failure of this abortive relationship is the crisis that impels the increasingly nervous Bickle into isolation, psychosis and armed mayhem. From this point on, for De Niro, desire is inescapably linked to violence. This leads to his obsessive, military-style preparation for the forthcoming apocalypse – though he still seems unsure, at this stage, precisely what this apocalypse will entail:

"June 29th: I gotta get in shape now. Too much sitting is ruining my body. Too much abuse has gone on for too long. From now on, it will be fifty push-ups each morning, fifty pull-ups. There'll be no more pills, there'll be no more bad food, no more destroyers of my body. From now on, it will be total organization. Every muscle must be tight."

Some critics found this aspect of the film to be inauthentic. Richard Schickel, for example, writing in *Time*, argued that:

"Travis's failure [with Betsy] as presented is more farcical than tragic, and it never adequately explains his becoming a killer... [**Taxi Driver**] is all too heavy with easy sociologizing to be truly moving... It is a conflict [Scorsese] can resolve only in a violence that seems forced and – coming after so much dreariness – ridiculously pyrotechnical."[20]

In fact, the precise form this act of violence takes is essentially irrelevant. What matters is its ritual significance, its purgative function, its power to release the now wild-eyed Bickle from the violent pressures of his urban neurosis. His murderous rampage is essentially an attempt to affront his own state of alienation and affirm that there is a certainty, an order that exists outside it. It is an attempt to exorcise his empty, tormented life, to enact his own, cathartic salvation, to stand up "against the scum, the cunts, the dogs, the filth, the shit". His shooting spree in the brothel is a primitive act of sacrificial mayhem, of spiritual cleansing through bloodshed, of regeneration through violence[21]. It is also an attempt to do something for which he will finally be recognized, to teach the "fuckers" and "screwheads" that "here's a man who would not take it any more... a man who stood up against the scum...".

Incidentally, many critics also rejected the violence towards the end of the film as excessive, overdone, even angering. Judith Crist in the *Saturday Review*, for example, described it (somewhat ignorantly) as "one of the most

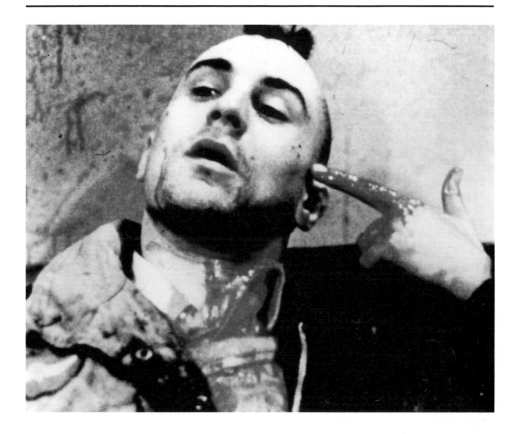

revolting outbursts of blood ever to splatter a non-'martial arts' movie"[22].

After his slaughterous rampage is over, Travis makes a futile attempt to shoot himself in the neck, but the guns click empty. Instead, his face contorted into a sober grimace, he helplessly raises a blood-soaked, dripping finger to his head and makes explosive sounds with his mouth, as he mimics pulling the trigger three times in a mock-suicide, then slowly loses consciousness as his head falls backwards. More than anything else, this final gesture seems to indicate the essentially symbolic, cleansing, purifying nature of the entire blood ritual.

"WE ARE THE PEOPLE"

The irony of De Niro's situation is that when he does manage to communicate his neurotic feelings through violence, society and the newspapers absolve him of his sins and praise him for his bloody sacrifice and vigilante bravery, according him celebrity status. Partaking of Bickle's own psychosis, society applauds the psychopathic assassin for his attempts to clean

up the filth of the city through an act of monumental slaughter. Consequently, it seems, however severely alienated from his society, De Niro is also, paradoxically, representative of the society, and his private urban neurosis is therefore symptomatic of a more general social malaise[23]. It is therefore perfectly if ironically appropriate that Bickle is ultimately, although temporarily, acclaimed as a hero by this sick society in which he lives:

"'I don't know which of us is crazier', Iris says to Travis at one point, 'me or you'. Once we in the audience are willing to make the same admission, we appreciate just how ominously ironic Pallantine's blandly optimistic election slogan really is. 'We Are the People', it says, and so we are – all of us, including the Travis Bickles around us and within us."[24]

The purgative act of violence, however, clearly offers no lasting solution. Nothing has changed. American society remains a wasteland, characterized by "dysfunctionality, moral degradation, corruption, violence, alienation and impotence"[25]. Travis Bickle must return to the streets, unpurged of his alienation, moral outrage, and urban neurosis.

CODA: JOHN W HINCKLEY JR – DEMENTIA SUBURBIA

In many ways, it's hard to imagine anyone less similar to Travis Bickle than John W. Hinckley Jr. Born in Ardmore, Oklahoma in 1955, Hinckley is the third child of a wealthy and prominent family. When John is four, the Hinckleys move to Dallas, and in 1973, after he graduates from high school, they moved to Evergreen, Colorado, not far from Denver, where John Hinckley Sr. establishes a new headquarters for the family oil business, the Vanderbilt Energy Corporation. John Jr. is brought up in a large suburban home, with a swimming pool in the back yard, and a private soda fountain. The prosecutor at his trial describes him as nothing more than "a bored young man with a lot of money"[26].

On March 30th 1981, Hinckley shoots and wounds President Ronald Reagan as the President is walking to his limousine at the Hilton Hotel, Washington D.C. Three other people are hit by Hinckley's bullets. One of them, Press Secretary James Brady, is gravely injured by a wound in the head. The shooting is observed by scores of eyewitnesses and seen by millions of others on television. Hinckley is immediately apprehended by federal law enforcement officers.

Upon examination, it is revealed that Hinckley has an obsession with Scorsese's **Taxi Driver**, which he has seen over fifteen times. Identifying with the character of Travis Bickle, Hinckley claims that his assassination attempt is a desperate act of love devoted to the actress Jodie Foster. It also becomes clear that Hinckley's own psychological symptoms betray less of Bickle's violent and dramatic urban neurosis than a rather more pathetic condition that soon comes to be known as dementia suburbia.

"AN OUTCAST IN THE MIDST OF MADNESS"[27]

What perhaps leads Hinckley to identify with the nervous Travis Bickle is his own sense of alienation from those around him. From high school on, Hinckley has no meaningful personal relationships outside his family, hanging out in fast food places and supermarkets[28]. He doesn't date, and has difficulty establishing peer relationships. After enroling in Texas Tech in Lubbock in the Autumn of 1973, he apparently spends much of his time for the next two years reading, watching television, listening to music and playing the guitar. Unlike Robert De Niro's battle-scarred Vietnam vet, however, Hinckley continues to live in the comfort of his parents' home, cutting something of a pathetic figure, according to his mother:

"[He] simply moped around in his room down on the ground floor, listening to old Beatles records and playing with the cat. He didn't want to meet people his own age in Evergreen, didn't want to play tennis, wouldn't even go for a walk with me."[29]

Also unlike Travis Bickle, John Hinckley receives the attentions of his father's company psychiatrist, Dr. John Hopper, to whom he confesses that "I have remained... inactive and reclusive over the past five years", and "I have managed to remove myself from the real world"[30]. Hopper considers Hinckley to be no different from many other suburban young people he's treated – lethargic, irresponsible, and lacking clear-cut goals for his life[31]. Defense lawyers at the trial make much of Hinckley's "flat affect" – an inability to respond to emotional stimuli in an appropriate fashion, a numbing or muting of emotions. They also claim that for many years, the media have provided Hinckley's only reality, replacing the flesh and blood contacts he seems incapable of forming. On top of this, the defense team produces a list of additional psychological symptoms which Hinckley has apparently been manifesting for the last five or six years. These include:

"... a pattern of unstable interpersonal relationships; an identity disturbance manifested by uncertainty about several issues relating to identity, namely self-image and career choice... chronic feelings of emptiness or boredom... secretiveness, jealousy... failure to accept societal norms; lack of self-confidence... several obsessive-compulsive traits... feelings of cool indifference and marked feelings of inferiority, shame, and emptiness in response to perceptions of defeat and failure; and the presence in interpersonal relationships of feelings of entitlement, alternating between extremes of over-idealization, interpersonal exploitativeness and devaluation and lack of empathy..."[32]

These are, of course, all symptoms which could also be applied to Travis Bickle in **Taxi Driver**, but with a significant distinction in cause and origin. In De Niro's case, his malaise derives from over-exposure to the horrors of urban life. Hinckley's condition, on the other hand, is a result of boredom, apathy, indifference, and privilege – the cumulative effect of living with his family for twenty-five years in the American suburbs.

"THE LOSER OF THE ONE-MAN RACE"

Just as Robert de Niro's Travis Bickle grows obsessed with doing something for which he will be recognized by the "fuckers" and "screwheads" around him, so Hinckley is morbidly self-attentive to his own place in history. In the autobiography he composed at the request of psychiatrist John Hopper, he wrote "I stayed by myself in my apartment and dreamed of future glory in some undefined field, perhaps music or politics"[33]. Defense psychiatrists describe him as suffering from a narcissistic personality disorder manifested by "a grandiose sense of self-importance and uniqueness (with exaggerations of achievements and talents); preoccupation with fantasies of unlimited success and ideal love; the search for constant attention"[34]. His introspective poetry betrays a Bickle-like need for recognition, to be achieved by means of some unspecified but world-shattering act of vengeance:

"See that living legend over there?
With one little squeeze of this trigger
I can put that person at my feet
Moaning and groaning and pleading with God...
This gun gives me pornographic power.
If I wish, the president will fall
And the world will look at me in disbelief."

Hinckley also testifies to a long-standing interest in the history of assassinations from Lincoln to Lennon, and seems particularly fascinated by the fame and publicity associated with various assassins, and assassination attempts[35]. Like Bickle, Hinckley also keeps a journal of his bleak, restless life, and sometimes records Bickle-like monologues into his tape recorder. One of these, his New Year's message "for the end of 1980 coming upon 1981", is played in court at his trial, and includes references to John Lennon, Jodie Foster, insanity and suicide. Lincoln Caplan describes it as "a lugubrious, self-conscious rambling, filled with clichés, threats, prissy stand-ins for obscenities, and dull comments on personal matters... the monologue revealed Hinckley as miserable, sad and wanting"[36] – quite a distinction from Bickle's tortured yet insightful and accurate diatribes. Interestingly enough, during the making of **Taxi Driver**, Paul Schrader read the published diary of Arthur Bremer – the man who shot Alabama Governor George Wallace, paralyzing him for life – out loud into a tape recorder. Although the script for **Taxi Driver** was written before the Bremer diary was published, Schrader claims that he was "very tempted to take some of the good stuff from it and add it to **Taxi Driver**, but I decided not to, because of legal ramifications"[37].

In the Spring of 1976 – the year **Taxi Driver** is released – Hinckley drops out of college and goes to Hollywood, where he spends six months in pursuit of a career as a songwriter – something of a futile endeavour, since his musical knowledge is virtually minimal. His letters home during the following two years seem consciously based on those written by Bickle to his parents in **Taxi Driver**. Travis, for example, chooses a cheap, kitschy card which reads "Happy Anniversary to a Couple of Good Scouts", and pictures a couple dressed like Boy Scouts on the front. Hinckley chooses a similarly kitschy card to send to his own parents, featuring a contrite and apprehensive-looking skunk, which reads "At times I've been a STINKER, in fact a PEST indeed...". Travis's message inside his card reads "I hope this card finds you all well as it does me". Hinckley's begins "I hope this card finds you both well and in good spirits".

Bickle explains that he's currently employed in a secret post by the government, and "making lots of money". Hinckley claims (falsely) that he's had a number of appointments with producers at MGM Records and United Artists who are "impressed" with his music, and want to get "professional musicians" to record some of his songs "for a demo tape". Bickle claims that he's "been going with a girl for several months and I know you would be proud if you could see her". Hinckley also creates his own glamorous fictional girlfriend, whom he calls "Lynn Collins". John tells his parents that he first met Lynn Collins in a launderette, that she's a wealthy young actress vacationing in California, and that "she seems to care about my career as much as her own"[38]. Later he claims to be spending Christmas in New York with Lynn, when he's actually sitting alone in his bedroom in Lubbock, Texas. During his trial, he claims that what prompted this creation of a fictitious girlfriend to write home about was Bickle's obsession with Betsy in **Taxi Driver**. Pathetically enough, the inept young Hinckley's identification with Travis Bickle extends even to a deliberate imitation of Bickle's own fantasies, failings and delusions.

"I FOLLOW THE LONG LOST SWINE"

Like Bickle, Hinckley soon begins stockpiling his own arsenal of weapons and ammunition, still with no particular target in mind. Travis purchases an assortment of four semi-automatic guns for $875 from an underground dealer – a .44 Magnum, a .38 Snubnose, a Colt .25 automatic and a .380. The movie's soundtrack explodes with the sound of the practice shots he fires at a target in an indoor range with his arsenal of illegal guns. In August 1970, John Hinckley buys a .38 caliber pistol at the Galaxy Pawn Shop in Dallas. In January 1980, he has his first "anxiety attack" and undergoes medical tests for dizziness. The same month, he purchases a 6.5 caliber rifle from Snidely Whiplash's Pawn Shop for $105. He also buys two boxes of bullets, including the exploding-head Devastators (which he refers to as "stingers") he would use in the assassination attempt. On July 10th, the doctors prescribe Valium for him to try. On July 16th he buys a .22 caliber rifle from the Galaxy Pawn Shop. On July 17th, the doctor prescribes Valium for six weeks. On October 11th he buys two more .22 caliber pistols and two boxes of shells, plus another .38, and registers at a rifle-and-pistol range near his parents' home in Evergreen, Colorado.

His private arsenal assembled, Travis Bickle begins stalking Senator Pallantine at various election rallies. Wearing a green army fatigue jacket and combat boots, his head shaved into a spiky mohawk, Bickle cuts a spooky and intimidating figure. Filling the stereotypical profile for a lone, crazed gunman, he's very quickly marked by Secret Service agents, who chase him through the crowd.

Similarly, Hinckley stalks both Carter and Reagan before his assassination attempt in March 1981. On the 30th September 1980, he takes a bus to Dayton, Ohio, where President Carter is visiting, decides not to shoot him, puts his guns in a locker and shakes Carter's hand at the convention center. In fact, during Hinckley's trial, the jury is shown television footage of Carter's visit to Dayton, with stop-action shots of John's face in the crowd, pressing to shake the President's hand. On the 7th October, he flies to Nashville, Tennessee, where Carter is due on the 9th, but again decides against an attempt on his life. Two weeks before Reagan is due in Washington, Hinckley flies out to the capital and has himself photographed in front of Ford's Theatre, where Lincoln was assassinated. After Reagan's arrival, Hinckley stalks the President, on one occasion carrying a gun, and sees him several times before the assassination attempt. Clearly, long before his assault on the President, Hinckley, like Travis Bickle, is what the prosecution refers to as "a hunter and a stalker"[39].

Bickle's response to the psychosexual crisis caused by Betsy's rejection is to stalk Senator Pallantine, with the intention of making his name as a political assassin. Frustrated in his efforts to get within firing range of Pallantine, he decides instead to "rescue" Iris from her low-life pimp, Sport, leading to the violent shootout at the brothel. For Hinckley, however, the crisis works the other way round. His assassination attempt is a displacement of his frustrated attempt to "rescue" Jodie Foster from her dorm room at Yale.

Hinckley's obsession with Foster begins in 1976, when he watches **Taxi Driver** over fifteen times, and develops in intensity over the next four years. After the death of John Lennon in 1980, Hinckley's feelings about Foster begin to spiral out of control. In October and November of this year, he begins stalking her at Yale University in New Haven, delivering poems and love-letters which Jodie throws away, followed by a batch of letters that she describes as "distressed-sounding", which she turns over to the Dean of her college. Hinckley also manages to speak to her a couple of times on the phone, when she dismisses him with polite but firm rebuttals. He also leaves her a note telling her "Just wait. I'll rescue you very soon. Please co-operate".

"Here comes 1981", says Hinckley into his tape recorder on New

Year's Ever 1980. "It's going to be insanity, even if I make it through the first few days. Anything I do in 1981 would be solely for Jodie Foster's sake. I want to tell the world in some way that I worship and idolize her. One of my idols was murdered and now Jodie's the only one left"[40]. At this point he seems to be on the verge of an extreme crisis. "My mind was on the breaking point," he writes later in his journal. "A relationship I had dreamed about went absolutely nowhere. My disillusionment with EVERYTHING was complete". He confessed to feeling "totally rejected" by Foster. The trips back and forth to New Haven he called "a month of unparalleled emotional exhaustion", and adds that if he fails to win Jodie's affection on his next trip, it will be "suicide city". His family begin to notice increasingly strange patterns of behaviour; his parents describe a situation at the dinner table when John simply hangs his head and sits limply for a few minutes before standing up in silence and walking away from the table[41]. His mental state at this time is precarious and apocalyptic; his psychiatrist describes it as "one of despair, depression, and a sense of the end of things".[42]

Early in March 1981, Hinckley travels once more to see Jodie Foster at New Haven in a last ditch effort to win her affection. He apparently believes that he has "some responsibilities toward her in terms of protecting her"[43], considering her to be "a prisoner at Yale"[44]. His "rescue attempt" is apparently intended to gain Jodie's "love and admiration", and "establish a relationship" with her[45]. When he gets to New Haven, he signs himself in at a motel under the name of "J. Travis". But when he tries to visit Foster at her dorm, he is unable even to gain admittance, or to get through to her on the telephone. The realities of Hinckley's life stubbornly refuse to conform to the movie script, and he flies back to Washington in a state of tremendous frustration and despair.

After Hinckley is arrested outside the Hilton Hotel in Washington, a letter is found in his room, addressed to Foster. "Dear Jodie," he writes:

"....As you well by now, I love you very much. The past seven months I have left you dozens of poems, letters, and messages in the faint hope you would develop an interest in me... Jodie, I'm asking you please look into your heart and at least give me the chance with this historical deed to gain your respect and love..."[46]

"REGARDLESS OF DISNEYLAND"

Like Bickle, Hinckley takes to wearing sunglasses, a green army fatigue jacket and a pair of black, metal-ringed, pull-on army boots. Unlike Bickle, however, Hinckley gets his doting mother to come shopping with him, to pick out and pay for his new outfit, which she describes as "an outlandish get-up", and can't understand why he needs combat boots for a visit to New Haven, where John has told her he's enroled in a creative writing course[47]. Like Bickle, Hinckley takes to drinking peach brandy. Unlike Bickle, however, the normally teetotal Hinckley asks his long-suffering mother to buy him a bottle on her next trip to the grocery store, which she does gladly, figuring she "could use the rest of it in cooking"[48]. Like Bickle, Hinckley is photographed holding a gun to his head in a staged mock-suicide. Unlike Bickle, however, Hinckley, morbidly obese at this stage, takes the picture himself, with an expensive time-release camera – and there are no bullets in his gun. He also seems to be deliberately acting like Bickle during his trial, shifting in his seat restlessly, twiddling his thumbs, tapping them together, rubbing his forehead with both hands, rolling his eyes and smiling wryly out of the side of his mouth.

To great consternation and notoriety, of course, John W. Hinckley Jr. is found "not guilty by reason of insanity" at his trial in 1982. Psychiatrists for both the defense and the prosecution spend hundreds of hours interviewing Hinckley to ascertain his state of mind at the moment of the shooting. Defense psychiatrists diagnose him as suffering from a major depressive disorder and from "process schizophrenia", a disorder marked by breaks from reality, magical thinking, and ideas of reference strong enough to be delusions – the belief that normal events, like President Reagan waving or Jodie Foster appearing on television, are happening just for him. He's also diagnosed as suffering from "recurrent thoughts of death and suicide", "dried-up emotions", "jumping thoughts" and a "narcissistic personality". All defense witnesses testify that Hinckley is "psychotic at the time of the offense"[49].

An important issue of debate at the trial is whether or not Hinckley actually "believed himself" to be Travis Bickle. According to Dr. William Carpenter Jr., one of the psychiatric experts on the defense team, Hinckley "identified" with Travis Bickle and "picked up in largely automatic ways many [of his] attributes". In Carpenter's opinion, this process, which was mainly an unconscious one, occurred because Hinckley's emotional isolation and poorly developed sense of identity made him especially "vulnerable" and "open to influences" at this time[50]. Lacking conviction about his own identity, Hinckley snatched fragments of identity from De Niro's rambling loner, gradually "becoming" Travis Bickle. Inevitably, Carpenter is closely cross-examined on this point by one of the prosecution team, Mr. Adelman, first in reference to Hinckley's "stalking" of President Carter on October 2nd, 1980:

Adelman: Did [Hinckley] think he was Travis Bickle on October 2nd in Dayton?

Carpenter: He had important aspects of Travis Bickle as part of his make-up through this identification process.
Adelman: Not my question, not my question.
Carpenter: He did not think, literally, believe that he was Travis Bickle. What he was doing was finding himself with many attributes of Travis Bickle and content...
Judge: (interrupting) Doctor, on this date in question, did he consider – did he think that he was Travis Bickle?
Carpenter: No. He experienced himself living out things from the Travis Bickle scenario. He did not literally believe himself to be Travis Bickle.

The same set of questions is asked in relation to Hinckley's arrest for possession of several guns at Nashville airport the following week:

Adelman: What I am asking you is are you aware that Mr. Hinckley gave information to the police upon arrest?
Carpenter: Yes.
Adelman: And he didn't say he was Travis Bickle when he was talking to the police, did he?
Carpenter: No.
Adelman: He told them he was John W. Hinckley Jr., correct?
Carpenter: Correct.

And the issue comes up a third time in relation to the assassination attempt itself:

Adelman: ....on this occasion did he think he was Travis Bickle?
Carpenter: The same situation as I described before.
Adelman: Well, can you tell us, yes or no, did he think he was Travis Bickle?
Carpenter: He found himself living out parallels of Travis Bickle. He did not believe himself to be Travis Bickle.

Commenting on the Hinckley case, Paul Schrader claims that the influence **Taxi Driver** had on Hinckley "doesn't mean we should start banning art, because if we did, there would be just as many psychopaths. Perhaps more"[51]. Scorsese also claims that he has no regrets about having made **Taxi Driver**. "It was not an irresponsible act – it was a responsible one," he claims. "Bob [De Niro] and I both thought so at the time. We both thought, this is something we're attracted to – let's go for it! Movies don't kill people. People kill people."[52]

"A FADED FLAG ON A WINDY DAY"

In the end, of course, American society responds to Hinckley's assassination attempt the same way it responds to Bickle's murderous acts of carnage: it makes him a star. The ironies of this fact are not lost on Hinckley himself, who tells his psychiatrist how thrilled he is to find that his name, like that of Travis Bickle, has gone from "totally nothing" to publication in thousands of newspapers[53]. "Since the shooting," claim his parents, "John has developed an unattractive obsession for notoriety. He likes to see himself in the news. He has elements of grandiosity and narcissism in his personality that are offensive to us all"[54]. More significantly, perhaps, Hinckley quickly came to believe that his attempt on the life of the President actually achieved everything he's ever dreamed of by linking his name permanently with that of Jodie Foster. Writes Hinckley:

"At one time Miss Foster was a star and I was the insignificant fan. Now everything is changed. I am Napoleon and she is Josephine. I am Romeo and she is Juliet. I am John Hinckley Jr. and she is Jodie Foster. I may be in prison and she may be making a movie in Paris or Hollywood, but Jodie and I will always be together, in life and death."[55]

And just as the name of John W. Hinckley Jr. will always be linked to that of Jodie Foster, so Robert De Niro's compelling performance as Travis Bickle will be always linked to the name of the notorious assassin it purportedly inspired. "God does indeed work in mysterious ways," claims Hinckley in a speech prepared to be read at his sentencing. "My life has become a melodrama. My past has been studied and analyzed not only by psychiatrists, but also by a large part of the general public[56]." And whilst some might find the media attention paid to Hinckley to be both redundant and offensive, an understanding of the parallels between Hinckley's own life and his fascination with **Taxi Driver** can help illuminate the complexity of De Niro's compelling performance as Travis Bickle. It also suggests something of the perverse tendencies of contemporary American culture, where a filmic portrayal of urban neurosis can be so readily transformed into a bona fide case of dementia suburbia.

NOTES

1. See Lincoln Caplan, *The Insanity Defense And The Trial Of John W. Hinckley, Jr.*, David Godine, Boston, Mass. 1984: 70.

2. See David Boyd, "Prisoner Of The Night", *Film Heritage* 1976–7, 12:2, 24–30.

3. See Richard Martin, *Mean Street And Raging Bulls – The Legacy Of Film Noir In Contemporary American Cinema*, Scarecrow Press, Lanham, Md., & London, 1997:81.

4. In fact, screenwriter Paul Schrader claims that it was when he was wandering around New York alone at night that the metaphor for **Taxi Driver** hit him. Schrader's own deep despair at the time – leading to obsessive behaviour, regular visits to porno theatres and recurrent fantasies of violence and suicide – brought him to the metaphor of "the man who will take anybody any place for money; the man who moves through the city like a rat through the river; the man who is constantly surrounded by people, yet has no friends; that was my symbol, my metaphor. This film is about a car as the symbol of urban loneliness, a metal coffin". Cit in Keith McKay, *Robert De Niro: The Hero Behind The Masks*, St. Martin's Press, New York: 1986, 44.

5. Boyd, 25.

6. Cit in McKay, 45.

7. Cit in Douglas Brode, *The Films Of Robert De Niro*, Citadel Press, New York: 1993, 1.

8. Ibid.

9. All reviews cit. in Brode, 103.

10. David Weaver, "The Narrative Of Alienation: Martin Scorsese's **Taxi Driver**", *CineAction!* Summer/Fall 1986: 14.

11. Richard Martin points out that **Taxi Driver** is the first instalment in a trilogy of neo-noir films scripted and directed by Paul Schrader, all featuring the existential loner hero. The trilogy is completed by **American Gigolo** (1980) and **Light Sleeper** (1991).

12. Weaver, 13.

13. See Boyd, 27.

14. Martin, 87.

15. Boyd, 29.

16. Martin, 84.

17. Ibid., 89.

18. Martin points out that Scorsese briefly discusses the framing in this scene in his audio

commentary on the **Taxi Driver** laser disc, side 1, chapter 11.

19. See Larry Gross, "Film Après Noir", *Film Comment* 12:4, 1976, 44–49.

20. Cit in Brode, 98.

21. See Julian Rice, "Transcendental Pornography And **Taxi Driver**", *Journal Of Popular Film* 5:2 (1976), 113.

22. Cit in Brode, 99.

23. See Boyd, 29.

24. Ibid, 30.

25. Martin, 89.

26. See Jack and Jo Ann Hinckley with Elizabeth Sherrill, *Breaking Points*, Chosen Books, Grand Rapids, MI 1985: 323.

27. All sub-headings in this section are lines of Hinckley's poetry, cit in Hinckley and Sherrill, 195–7.

28. See Caplan, 91.

29. Hinckley and Sherrill, 17.

30. Ibid., 291.

31. Ibid., 290.

32. Cit in Caplan, 70.

33. Ibid., 34.

34. Ibid., 70.

35. See Peter W. Low, John Calvin Jeffries Jr. and Richard J. Bonnie, *The Trial Of John W. Hinckley Jr: A Case Study In The Insanity Defense*, Foundation Press, Inc., Mineola, NY, 1986: 61.

36. Cit in Caplan, 17.

37. Cit in McKay, 49.

38. Cit in Hinckley and Sherrill, 93.

39. Cit in Caplan, 8.

40. Cit in Hinckley and Sherrill, 303.

41. Cit in Low et al., 99.

42. Ibid., 33.

43. See Caplan, 76.

44. Ibid., 91.

45. See Hinckley and Sherrill, 169.

46. Ibid., 169.

47. Ibid., 98, 126.

48. Ibid., 150.

49. Cit in Low et al, 27.

50. Cit in Low et al, 24.

51. Cit in McKay, 53.

52. Cit in Patrick Agan, *Robert De Niro – The Man, The Myth And The Movies*, Robert Hale, London 1989, 48.

53. See Caplan, 58.

54. Cit in Hinckley and Sherrill, 346–7.

55. Ibid., 341.

56. Cit in Caplan, 101.

ROBERT DE NIRO IN
'RAGING BULL'

DYNAMIC DUO

If there is nothing else that can be said for it, Martin Scorsese's classic boxing biopic **Raging Bull** has, at the very least, gone the distance. In his cinema round-up of the decade in *The Guardian*, Derek Malcolm cited the film as among the most important American movies of the '80s, while in the June '99 issue of *Maxim*, **Raging Bull** made number seven in their "50 Films You Must See" feature, believing it to be "Scorsese's ultimate guy movie". To say that it is a biopic *par excellence*, a crucial contender for the top '80s US movie and the director's most complete statement on machismo, is perhaps telling less than half of the story.

Above all, it may be the moment when two creative whirlwinds merged and met each other at the peak of their artistic climb. Robert De Niro had starred in three Martin Scorsese pictures prior to **Raging Bull**. 1973's **Mean Streets**, **Taxi Driver** from 1976 and **New York, New York** a year later. As wonderful as those films are, their venture into the ring was as complete a meeting of two individual talents as modern cinema can recall.

Of course, much has been made about the De Niro preparation for the film – his work-outs in the gym made him lean and hungry for the role of the young ambitious fighter, while his weight gain of over fifty pounds left him bloated and swollen reflecting the consumptive and obsessive personality and lifestyle of the older Jake La Motta with his career over and his life struggling to stay intact.

And that union was rewarded with a joint trip to the Oscars ceremony of 1981, Scorsese with a Best Director award to fight for and De Niro in the Best Actor category. One of them was to walk away with a trophy but destiny was not to shine for Scorsese. The combination of De Niro's raw performance and his commitment to his art were more than enough to fend off the opposition. The pair's working relationship was never quite the same afterwards. Certainly, they still had memorable cinematic moments to share – **Goodfellas**, **Casino** and **King Of Comedy** being three notable future collaborations – but both their careers seemed slowly to be taking different routes.

De Niro, in particular, was to become less reliant on his mentor and made films under the tutelage of directors as diverse as Roland Joffe (**The Mission**), Brian De Palma (**The Untouchables**) and Kenneth Branagh (**Mary Shelley's Frankenstein**). Yet, looking back, can De Niro claim to have been more in his element than in those early projects with Scorsese and, in

particular, the experience of **Raging Bull** – when pulling a punch was never an option?

SYNOPSIS

New York City in 1964, and an ageing and bloated ex-boxer, Jake La Motta is rehearsing his lines before going on stage to what may or may not be a welcoming audience. Chomping on his cigar, the gags, the puns and the wordplay are coming together slowly and fitfully, his mind tired and literally punch-drunk after his years of abuse in and out of the ring.

We flash back to 1941, the location the Cleveland Arena. La Motta is up against Jimmy Reeve and is losing the bout on points. He badly needs a knock-out as the contest approaches its final moments and in a fury of punches, he gets it. Unfortunately, it is too close to the final bell and despite leaving his opponent flat out and shell-shocked, La Motta loses the fight on a technicality. As the announcement makes its way through the auditorium, a riot breaks out around the ring. Tables and chairs are thrown through the air and spectators race around, either to get away or involved in the mayhem. An early indication in the film that violence is to follow La Motta everywhere, both within and without his chosen workplace.

La Motta's brother Joey (Joe Pesci) is seen chatting to Salvy (Frank Vincent), a member of The Mob who informs him that Jake's loose-cannon behaviour is causing some concern within the higher echelons of the organisation and that Joey should keep a tighter rein on him. From there, Joey walks in to a scene of domestic non-bliss as Jake and his first wife are having one of their many showdowns over as insignificant a detail as the proper cooking of a steak. This sets the scene for the pettiness and awkward nature of much of Jake's dealings with everyone.

Joey and Jake are next seen sparring together in the gym. The Mob's presence upsets both and the sparring turns into a scrap before we see the brothers relaxing by the pool and Jake has his first glimpse of his future wife, Vickie (Cathy Moriarty). Jake insists on knowing her but Joey is reluctant to pass on any information about her, knowing that she is close to The Mob. The brothers go on a night out, to the dismay of Jake's wife – this appears to be the last straw for her as we now witness her last appearance in the film. They are off to an annual church dance, of all places – more gangster connections – yet violence even spills out here.

On a later occasion, Joey introduces Vickie to Jake and they go for a drive, ending up back at Jake's place where a love sparring match begins – intimacy and communication are at a premium, but a connection has been made. It's now 1943 and La Motta is beginning to fulfil the promise and the faith which has been invested in him as he takes on, knocks down and finally

defeats Sugar Ray Robinson. Now, Jake and Vickie are a strong item but he is determined to keep his career on track and her amorous advances are, almost, put in check. La Motta and Robinson meet again in Detroit and despite being knocked to the canvas by La Motta, Robinson wins on points. This setback makes Jake even more determined and we see snapshots of his next six fights (all victories) intercut with colour footage of Jake and Joey playing happy families with their wives and children.

Of course, all this apparent bliss is a sheen and the next scene is more typical – Jake and Joey both bullying their wives as the pair plot Jake's next move, a fight with the young pretender, Janiro. One innocent remark from Vickie about Janiro's good looks is enough to set La Motta off on a jealousy rant, but soon he is off to prepare for his next bout with a warning to Joey to keep an eye on Vickie in his absence. His brother does just that, but at the Copacabana club, things get out of hand when Joey has a vicious fight with Salvy, who comes out of it much the worse after Joey repeatedly slams a car door on his head.

Mob leader Tommy Como (Nicholas Colosanto) brings Salvy and Joey together at the Debonair Social Club and all appears forgiven, but Joey is given a warning to keep an eye on his brother. Thinly veiled threats about fight-fixing are made and in his bout with Billy Fox at Madison Square Garden, only Jake's pride prevents him from taking the dive requested by the Mob. Despite La Motta's partly failed attempts at throwing the fight, the book is thrown at him and he is suspended. Two years later and he is back in the ring and getting close to having a chance at the middleweight crown. More victories are gained but his irrationally jealous nature is just as fervent.

At last he wins the middleweight championship of the world but just when he has it all, he loses it, accusing Joey of messing around with Vickie – "Did you fuck my wife? Did you fuck my wife?" etc. He attacks both of them and they react by removing themselves from his life. In Dauthille in 1950, Sugar Ray gets his title back from La Motta but only on points, and Jake taunts his conqueror at the end, berating him for being unable to knock him out.

La Motta is now in retirement and, seeking some purpose and new directions, opens up his own club, imaginatively titled "Jake La Motta's". At first things go well and he rides on a storm of public goodwill and patient tolerance. Even his third rate stand-up act goes down a treat. Eventually, his arrogance is his downfall as the booze takes its toll and he is arrested after two underage girls are found to be drinking in his club – could this be the Mob's final revenge?

Vickie leaves him and he tries to raise some bail money by selling his middleweight Belt. He is put in a cell where he takes his frustration out on the wall with his head and fists. It is now 1958 and he is back in the clubs,

but this time to unfriendly audiences and his second career has finally died. He meets his brother by accident and tries to make things up but Joey is too smart and has too long a memory to forgive him. Finally, we see Jake rehearsing in front of the mirror backstage and he is mimicking Brando's "coulda been a contender" speech, in which he absolves himself of any blame for his downfall.

GIRLS AND BOYS

Few directors, American or otherwise, have been so closely associated with the notion of what it is to be male than Martin Scorsese. His take on the psychology and physicality of maleness has driven his work – and both factors are at their peaks in **Raging Bull**. Odd then that the story of Jake La Motta and the possibilities it threw up for that state to be analysed was one which the director was apparently not too keen on, and it was Robert De Niro who was the instigator of the film's genesis, spending many a conversation trying to convince his friend and mentor that the terrain was ripe.

Eventually Scorsese complied, with the realisation that there was much to be told in a story which related as much to the director himself directly as it did to the themes involved. Scorsese had fallen ill after the long and tortuous process that was the making of **New York, New York** and he felt he was at a crossroads in both his life and his career.

The shooting of the film was to take him back to the scene of his childhood, the Lower East Side, and Jake and Vickie's wedding on a rooftop is modelled on Scorsese's parents' nuptials. That connection plus the feelings running through him that this next project, whatever it was to be, would be his last feature film meant that everything, or as much as he was capable of producing in his state of health, would be put in to **Raging Bull** to make it a classic. He even decided to shoot in black and white for posterity reasons – b/w stock lasts longer than colour and Scorsese wanted this film to last and be remembered – as well as a way of evoking the times and giving the film a sheen of class to accompany its depth of substance.

And what that dual energy of Scorsese and De Niro created was one of the most reprehensible creations of manhood ever committed to film. Even when considering De Niro's previous work with Scorsese, Jake La Motta was a vile character. In **Mean Streets**, Johnny Boy is nothing worse than a loveable rogue, Travis Bickle in **Taxi Driver** is a monster quite understandably created out of his scum-laden environment and, later on, even the loathsome Max Cady in **Cape Fear** can be considered a semi-innocent victim of the US legal system. Jake La Motta, though, is someone who leaves no quarter for sympathy – the obsessive jealousy which fuels his inability to connect, communicate or understand other people close to him is hard to see past. It loses him his career, his wife and his brother and leaves him a shambling wreck at the end of the film. Yet even here he finds it difficult to blame himself, always looking to others to point the finger at, as perfectly evoked in his final speech – recalling that he could have been a contender if it wasn't for all those hangers-on and leeches, ie. his loved ones who tried to run his life for him.

Yet, his single-mindedness or selfishness was hurting all those around him. Violence is never far from the surface with La Motta, whether it is of his own making or simply by the very fact that he is in the vicinity. So, at a church hall dance, a ruckus breaks out and his fighter instinct draws him to it – his over-inflated sense of superiority (while actually maintaining a giant inferiority complex) makes him feel that he can act as a peacekeeper, a guardian of justice. Brutal acts of violence are even carried out on his behalf – such as the moment when Joey (Joe Pesci) struggles to keep a lid on his misplaced loyalty to his brother, seeing the Mob with Vickie while Jake is off on fight duty. As with most acts of instinctive violence, this is an act which is to come back to haunt him.

And, as with much of Scorsese's output, there is an unresolved tension between men and women. La Motta's attitude to women is very much of his hard environment and social context – a tough, uncompromising negativity, their purpose being to serve, and hell hath fury for any female who tries to defy him or get in his way. And what better moment to signify this extended hostility than when the riot breaks out at the end of his unsuccessful fight at the beginning of the film – a riot which is partly due to the injustice of the verdict and partly as a result of La Motta's incitement of the crowd. As chairs fly and bones are broken, a woman is seen being trampled underfoot. This image perfectly sums up La Motta's attitude – he just can't help being rough on women who will be victims to both his direct and unwitting behaviour, as his first and second wives are all too readily to find out.

An argument over whether a steak has been done to his requirements is as grave as accusing a wife of infidelity. The same outcome exists – if you're not doing things Jake's way you'll better shape up or shift out. There is no evidence of a strong matriarchal figure in Jake and Joey's lives, so there is no sense of a gauge for the pair to measure their attitudes to women. Jake is as unstinting in his recklessness to them whether they are put-upon wives, respectable married women who he can pour a drink over because he is in his own environment of the club, or females he can treat as toys or objects for him to play with, as in the case of the two young girls who are ultimately his downfall.

Yet, Jake is as tunnel-visioned towards men as he is to his women. His jealousy destroys the close professional and personal link with his brother while his arrogance (or, if you're being kinder, puffed-up pride) towards his fellow pugilists leads him to taunt Sugar Ray Robinson despite losing his crown to him. The fact that La Motta failed to be knocked out was just as important to him than retaining his crown – what, after all, could be worse to his sense of manhood than being put on his pants in the ring. And near the end when he is put in a prison cell over the two under-age girls, Jake is unable to take his punishment without the rage boiling over, and he thumps his head against and smashes his fists into the cell wall.

PULLING NO PUNCHES

So, **Raging Bull** stands up well as another segment of the De Niro/Scorsese take on what it is to be a man but – and this may well have been one of the director's reservations over wanting to make the picture – does it stand up as a boxing film? Many of the codes and signifiers of boxing occur out of the ring – the raw violence is an obvious one, the shaping each other up around the kitchen table (beautifully detailed sparring, you could call it) between Jake and Vickie is perhaps less so, but equally as instructive. Their relationship

could be seen almost as a metaphor for what goes on in the ring – the early sizing up of one another from a distance, then up close before the real hostility sets in and all-out war rages.

Scorsese clearly didn't want his to be just another boxing film riddled with all the usual box-pic clichés. For those who have wished to put the sport on celluloid, it's seemed to be a safer bet to take the documentary approach. In recent times, there have been successful works such as **When We Were Kings**, Leon Gast's evocative and thrilling look at the Ali/Foreman bout, and surrounding mayhem, in Zaire 1974 and last year's **Southpaw** which followed the story of amateur Francis Barrett as he made his way from traveller outcast to Olympic hero.

Scorsese wanted both the truth of La Motta's story – which a documentary may have captured easily enough with old footage – but also the hyper-real sense of what a boxer thinks when in the ring. He wanted a close-up on the flying blood and the racing mind and only the fictional lens could see in there. What he must have feared and fought tooth and nail against was some of the existing shambolic and laughable attempts at re-enacting the inside of the ring – any of the **Rocky** films, any of the Elvis celluloid scraps or even the gloopy syrup of Zefirelli's **The Champ**. For a template of how to do it right, only the likes of Robert Wise's **The Set-Up** (1948) and John Huston's **Fat City** (1972) would be of any assistance to Scorsese.

The failure of Martin Scorsese to win the Best Picture Oscar of '81 is not something he would particularly have cared deeply about – getting to the end of a gruelling project such as **Raging Bull** is reward enough. And even better to create a work of art by utilising the best elements of a sub-genre (boxing movie) and adapting them to his own themes and fascinations. Perhaps, seeing his friend and colleague walking off with a gong would also have given the director just as much pleasure, too. De Niro's performance as Jake La Motta has become legendary. The weight gain and training regime with the boxer himself, earned De Niro much column inches, respect and iconic status as a genius of his art, one who is so obsessed with The Truth that extraordinary lengths need to be gone to.

Robert De Niro may even point to other roles which have given him more satisfaction in himself and his work, but his creation of a man teetering on the brink through his own failings and emotional flaws has been surpassed by few in modern cinema.

'KING OF COMEDY': DISRUPTED SIGNALS, BLURRED RECEPTION, FLATTENED IMAGE – TV's "BORDERLINE PERSONALITY" DISORDERED

"LET'S HEAR IT FOR..."

De Niro had been a virtuoso of the sick and thick, in **King Of Comedy** he made it *shtick* – "bits of business", show business in fact, a comic routine. In **Mean Streets**, De Niro's enigmatic Johnny Boy drives his reluctant brother's-keeper Charlie to theological distractions by his inexplicably erratic alternations between frustrating moronic and endangering psychotic trickster. In **Taxi Driver**, De Niro's Travis Bickle alternates fascinatingly from scene to scene between a profound bafflement regarding the dictates of cultural codes and the intuitive visionary recognitions which his creeping psychosis promotes; scenes of incomprehension – failure to anticipate Betsy's repulsion at pornography, failure to decipher Wizard's rambling, inarticulate oracle, or failure to comprehend Iris's complacent degradation – alternate with scenes of psychotically acute penetration into the sinister life of things as he contemplates the crumpled bill of the pimp or the drivelling babble of his TV or the provocative back-talk of his double in the mirror. So too in **Raging Bull**, alternating scenes captivate by dramatically depicting how the shadow-boxing Jake La Motta's stubborn, tenacious hold on self-esteem not only gives him the capacity to withstand beatings but, in as much as he sadomasochistically administers them to himself, also serves as his most formidable assailant, brutishly stupid paranoia striking faster than canniness can duck and weave.

But in **King Of Comedy**, there is no alteration, no punch(line) and counter-punch(line), but rather an ambiguous sustained conflation of sickness and thickness that uniquely defines De Niro's conception of the man who would be king – Rupert Pupkin. Each of the earlier characters have moments when they seem preternaturally dense, ambiguously sluggish or slow. Each, by selectively ignoring most of what is said to him or asked of him, and by registering only what will serve his purposes, manages to get under the skin of anyone who would exert their authority to deny him his will or heart's desire. And by virtue of this uncanny inertia, each to a remarkable degree compels others to reorient themselves and take up a position toward him and toward their habitual world that they would not otherwise have dreamt of taking. All three are to this degree, and quite despite their violent pugnacity or apocalyptic tonal register, comic characters. If De Niro plays Travis Bickle as kinetic inertia – once put in motion he stays in motion, as his first name suggests, and in this motion explosively catalyzes the pressurized angers and frustrations visibly steaming up from below the city surface through its "manhole covers" – he plays the more pedestrian Rupert Pupkin as less temperamentally mobile or mercurial. If Travis is an unstoppable force of accelerating velocity, then Rupert is the immovable object. De Niro plays him as opaque and thick-skinned and sedentary as the fruit which with his ridiculous name is often comically confused ("K" is always funny, a vaudeville axiom cracks wise). Alike in being extreme outsiders, onlookers always looking in, Travis and Rupert are most alike in their notably diminished psychological affect, the relatively narrow range and low key of their emotional register and its correlative psychic states. Both in their very odd ways are remarkably impassive until that moment, that ambiguous moment of breakdown and resolution that Americans call a "snap decision".

That said, De Niro's Rupert Pupkin is an extraordinary comic characterization almost unprecedented in performance history – probably the only distant approximations being the resiliently unaffected Chaplin and Keaton personae, who as clownish mutes survive brilliantly by their different genius for indifference, for seeming never to notice they are under assault or are being completely ignored as if they didn't exist at all. In the longer literary and folklore traditions, Pupkin's closest relatives might well be the beatific *schlemiels* of the Yiddish tradition, wise transcendently oblivious fools who stumble backward into heaven, or more recently, and deriving from this same Yiddish tradition, the eponymous "hero" of Jaroslav Hasek's early-20th century classic *The Good Soldier Schweik*, whose comic ambiguity drives his commanding officers mad because they can't definitively ascertain whether he is a cunning rogue or a moronic simpleton.

But what distinguishes "Rupert Pupkin" as a characterization is that his ambiguous conflation of sickness and thickness is fundamental to the thematic discourse that De Niro and Martin Scorsese, as collaborators, authorize and mobilize. The difficulty the audience has in deciding whether Rupert's narcissistic obliviousness is pathetic, admirably efficient, or sinister serves to define the essential nihilism of the culture industry into which he struggles to insinuate himself and which he finally comes to personify. The audience's difficulty in deciding – in diagnosing – also serves to define the nature of the audience constructed, with its own complicity, by that industry insofar as De Niro's performance compels the film's audience to experience and to want to resist the kind of deeply illusory relationship that television profits from constructing its audience to desire, expect, and be satisfied with.

King Of Comedy is a symptomatic diagnosis of a mass-mediated blankness upon which the audience is invited to project its own culturally-induced narcissistic phantasies. And the epitome, the personification, of this blankness is Rupert Pupkin. Empathize with Pupkin's pathos as the proverbial sad funny-man (due to a loneliness not unlike Travis Bickle's) or identify with his comically heroic, typically American struggles to be somebody, to be somebody not just anybody – as his cheering fictive television audience does at the end – and you become like him, delusively invested in the culture's endemic "bad faith". But view him from a distance as a case history and you the spectator may lose the possibility of recognizing your likeness in him as a fellow mass-media(ted) gawker, gawking even as you scrutinize and contemplate him as a symptomatic manifestation of a televisually communicable illness.

The remainder of this essay will consider the satirical use to which this brilliant characterization is put by Scorsese, as well as the psycho-social implications of De Niro's performance *shtick* insofar as these comic bits of business materialize and substantiate the split between show business and the business of showing. These bits of (show) business display an insider's view from the other side of the screen of the distracting light displayed by that screen, so that its brightness keeps forever inaccessible, and unseen, the fact that its ultimate, ambiguous function is to screen the spectators out.

"I SHALL ADHERE TO YOUR REQUEST, SIR..."

As the disembodied promise of the TV host bleeds over and fades into a backstage scene, a shifty-eyed dude looking like a Miami porn impresario cum lounge lizard (De Niro) slithers through a milling throng of autograph-seeking fans, looking for his opening, for his spot, as the fans like heat-seeking missiles converge upon their target, TV's reigning "king of comedy", Jerry Langford (Jerry Lewis), as he emerges from performance toward his waiting limo. The pop! pop! pop! of flashbulbs and bright bursts of flaring light establish the equation: cameras are as assaultive as guns, fans like assassins.[1] Now the latent violence suddenly erupts as a hysterical gibbering female fan (Sandra Bernhard) invades the confines of Langford's car and assaults him with her ardorous adoration. But Langford is saved, extricated by that very same shifty, weasel-faced dude, who locks the hysterical fan alone inside the limo. As her hands claw the car window, Scorsese freezes the frame: the credits roll over and right through the desperate outstretched fingers that would grasp the distant star beyond their reach. Suddenly the car window, lit by the spectral light of bulbs going nova, becomes a TV screen, but it's the same shifty dude centred within its frame, Langford for that frozen very long moment having been displaced to off-screen space. His beady eye squints

peek-a-boo through splayed fingers, looking back at the shut-in shut out, at the position of deprivation, the spectatorial position, having somehow miraculously passed over to where things glow.

      This brilliantly conceived credit-sequence does more than foreshadow the ultimate trajectory of the narrative, Scorsese's contemporary version of the archaic usurpation and uncrowning of the old king and the ritual installation of his successor. It also metaphorically articulates the symbolic meanings of social mediated space. For **King Of Comedy** is nothing if not a sardonic meditation on the reciprocal dialectical conditions and blurring unstable distinctions between being on the outside looking in and being on the inside seeming to look out, between being without and being within, between off and on stage. The dialectic and irony of the situation is implicit in the transparency of the car window in its capacity as a barrier. The transparent barrier keeps the undeserving from penetrating and reaching a special space, a space consecrated by the presence of the celebrity, but it permits the eyes the illusion of being there in that space with the special people whose presence there proves they deserve to occupy it. Not only does the transparency of the medium belie its character as a barrier, it disavows its character as a barrier by inviting the spectator, in the manner of certain shop windows, to reach out scopically to caress what on the other side can never be possessed. This dialectic of the presence of distance defines it as a borderline condition. This window that flares to a screen yet in so doing becomes a barrier whose very transparency disavows its true function is the first of the film's many spatialized evocations of the desire and frustration aroused and promoted at the media(ted) borderlines of our culture and of the "borderline" personalities who personify a once clinical condition that has now become socialized and virtually endemic and who are the only ones who can successfully negotiate and penetrate these patrolled borders because of their capacious incapacity for distinguishing between self and Other, here and Over There. This long-take on the desire to take and the inability to have inaugurates Scorsese's film-long metaphoric discourse on the nature of relationships in media-constructed late capitalism and the media's institutional remapping and regulation of social lived-space.

The subsequent abrupt convergence and forced intimacy between Langford and his erstwhile deliverer Rupert Pupkin in the backseat of the limo is conducted as a stylized struggle of contrasting wills to power, each applying its own artful stratagems of almost brutal courtesy. Played against the grain of his own manic-spastic persona, Lewis' Langford is cold, taciturn, almost morose, not so much restrained as virtually constrained by his taut body armour, which immobilizes even his jowls and neck. While De Niro's Pupkin displays how even obsequious ingratiation, when fuelled by delusional self-conviction, can become a weapon of assault ("I wouldn't be doing this if I wasn't absolutely convinced that I'm dynamite"). He more and more leans into and impinges on Langford's armorial formality and corseted courtesy, calling him to account with a shrewd eye to the price of demarcated, mediated social space ("I did put myself *on the line* for you"). Langford stiffly averts his face again and again in the face of an onslaught of wheedling ego that serves to substantiate the etymological link between fan and fanatic. He responds, much as a more weary Charlie might to a more brazen Johnny Boy, with formal avuncular counsel expressed in a slow calming tone meant to humour, moderate and contain the potential for violence that Pupkin represents to him. Not surprisingly his tensed counsel is all about rules, more pointedly the "ground rules" of "the business" intended to put the upstart in his place by first putting that sense of regulated space in his head, establishing it at the center of his cognitive map of how the social world is laid out. And that space for Pupkin, Langford assures him, is "the bottom": "'You got to start at the bottom.' 'I know, that's where I am, at the bottom.' 'Well, that's a perfect place to start.'" Whether regarding entry to his car or entry into the business or, as later, entry into his house, Langford's rules of admittance begin with a mandatory admission of unworthiness, and from there they are largely formulated in terms of ritual stages of a passage: a border crossing.

Through it all, swinging from obtuse impudence to oily exuberance and back again, Pupkin continues to display what may be his only authentic claim to genius: his utter impassivity and imperviousness to the subtextual messages inherent in the intonations of others (he never seems to notice, for example, the disparity between Langford's public performance of cheerful *bonhomie* and his off-stage unsmiling joylessness). This is a capacity, ultimately, for remaining undissuaded because he wears people down even faster than he wears out his welcome. In these terms, the scene on the steps of Langford's hotel might be compared to the scene in **Taxi Driver** in which Travis Bickle invades the institutional space of hegemonic power, the political campaign headquarters, to solicit the attentions of his chosen icon, from whom he will not take "no" for an answer either.[2] The spatial composition of the scene on the steps visibly stages the psycho-social divide between elites and plebs, dominants and their suitors, celebrities and their consumers, and the attempt to erase the boundaries of that divide. Langford stands atop a flight of steps, magisterially occupying in his stiffness a space reminiscent of a votive monument in relation to Rupert, his ostensible devotee at the foot of the steps. However, Pupkin's ambiguity as a suitor is codified by his suit coat. As a copy of Langford's his whole attire defines his imitativeness (proverbially, a mode of flattery), but as a "knock-off", as they say in media marketing, it identifies his perhaps as-yet unconscious willingness to be the cut-rate substitute that will aggressively drive the original from the cut-throat marketplace. He is already potentially a Brutus to his Caesar. Just to get rid of him, Langford finally agrees to listen to a tape of his stand-up comedy routine.

"THERE'S NO WAY WE CAN PROVE WE BELONG HERE"

Once Pupkin undertakes to get the tape through the bureaucratic labyrinth of corporate entertainment, he and the spectator both begin to experience, at their different levels of awareness, the spatial coordinates of hegemonic power. Some of the most authentically comic *shtick* in the film, certainly more genuinely funny than Pupkin's embarrassingly successful monologue, constitute bits of business that mock the structuring of space by big business. The coordinates of social space provide powerful dictates concerning the decorums of behaviour, and the film generates much of its comic pleasure from Pupkin's deconstruction and subversion of that space, those decorums. He refuses to be expelled permanently through the corporation's revolving doors, which as a lateral version of the Wheel of Fortuna, ancient symbol of the cycle of rise and fall, functions to define the instability of the categories of being in and being out, a success and a failure, wanted and unwanted. His repeated attempts to penetrate to the inner sanctum of power, prestige, and

self-satisfaction, Langford's office, are just as repeatedly foiled at the reception cubicle, whose transparent plasticine design seems to alternately frame both him and the receptionist as if they were on TV screens. Again, the prevaricating transparency of insurmountable barriers is correlated and supported by a mode of courteousness that is inhuman and almost brutal in its smooth flatness of tone and hollow signifiers of bright cheer, such as the equally plasticine smile of Langford's assistant producer. Both the architectural design and the demeanour of the staff semiotically convey and implement the "standards and practices" that ensure the "smooth functioning of our operation... our organization", as one corporate lackey puts it. The audience can only applaud Pupkin's indomitable obduracy in managing, if only for a few minutes, to render the slick organizational machinery a Keystone Cop chaos.

But much of the film's fascination is due to De Niro's decision to underplay his role in most scenes, most notably those involving the staff in the reception area of the Langford show and those involving the FBI. It is difficult to be certain whether Rupert's calm courteousness in the face of rejection, rejection at the reputed site of reception, reflects his obliviousness or his stubborn perseverance or his perversity. His tendency to speak in formal, grammatically precise sentences, a tendency he shares with Langford, seems diagnostically part of the same syndrome as his comical capacity for detachment from immediate environmental pressures. In keeping with the comic's characteristic play with the ambiguities of capacity and incapacity, this trait is made to seem indicative of a more disturbing, less benign form of psychological detachment, an amorphous, socially pervasive, culturally endemic detachment that Scorsese uses the exaggerative, amplifying strategies of satire to consolidate in the figure of Rupert Pupkin. Rupert's courteous, persevering insistence (and a gun) succeeds in making Langford and the TV network "adhere to [his] request", thereby actualizing the illusion of obedient servitude to the viewer's whimsical will that TV, as the most ostensibly friendly of entertainment media, strives to produce. It also actualizes the metaphorical implications suggested by the audial superimposition of that promise over Rupert's image, which had subtly served to intimate the reciprocal master-slave bonds that inextricably tie celebrities to fans and vice-versa.

Pupkin's realization that he must define the space of negotiation culminates with Langford being kidnapped and then bound with tape, which literalizes a metaphor in the conventional comic manner (Langford's staff had deflected Pupkin's advances by claiming their boss was "tied up" in meetings). As poetic justice, it also completes the stiff, constrained immobility already so advanced in Langford's personality. Pupkin demonstrates he too is not unaware of the ironic doublings of the situation. After Langford is hung up on as a poser, a prankster mimic, Pupkin observes that "They" have treated you like "They" treated me. Langford's momentary glimpse of himself as a bogus imitation of himself seems to stimulate a glimmer of awareness of what those like Pupkin have felt all their life: that "there's no way we could prove we belong here". This is an existential comment as much as a social one.

Pupkin's mirroring of Langford's attire in the earlier scene had constituted not just a cheap joke about the link between aspiration and imitation. It had also served to pointedly introduce at the level of plot and characterization the dominant thematic preoccupation of the film, a preoccupation determining the *mise-en-scène* and responsible for most of the ironic doublings within the narrative pattern, for the metaphoric implications of the imagery, and for the most ingenious camera work and editing. All of these converge to demonstrate some of the causes and some of the consequences of the contemporary instability of the sense of self, particularly as it relates to the dubious status (or questionable existence) of originality in the contemporary world of mass-produced copies, imitations, simulacra. Virtually all the details in the film – from the prevalence of reflecting surfaces

(mirrored doors and glass panelling, for example) to Masha's whiny protest that she "wants to be Black" (to be Tina Turner, her mass-mediated celebrity image of what being "Black" entails) – are organized into a prolonged meditation on the contemporary disintegration of the boundaries of a coherent self under the pressure of extreme aspirations for recognition and esteem exacerbated, if not caused, by the ubiquitous presence of the mass-media, epitomized by TV and the images of celebrity it provides for mass-consumption. The film focuses on the phenomena of mass-mediated images of celebrity and fan identification, desire, and aspiration in order to address how these phenomena have served to destabilize the individual's sense of being unique, of possessing a unique set of traits and attributes, which is the founding principle of American democratic ideology – and, paradoxically, of mass-marketing. Thus, when the loveless obsessive fan, Masha, equates having "Good old-fashioned, all-American fun!" with being "Out of my head!" her yearning serves to mark an historical passage across a border-line or divide. It also serves to suggest how the film's spatialized emphasis on the distinction between being within and being without and its blurring of the distinction between self and Other are two aspects of the same discursive strategy.

"I'M WITH YOU ALWAYS..."

The film deliberately blurs the supposed distinction between inside/outside by refusing to signal whether we are or are not inside the delusional fantasies of Rupert. In the scene in which Langford courts Pupkin to be his substitute, the signal is delayed and it is only by attending closely to Pupkin's clothes that the spectator can discern that the space in which this is happening is imaginary. This strategy might be seen as the equivalent of a principle of comedy Langford articulates for Pupkin: *do* the punchline, rather than announce you are about to do it. But the ultimate function of a scene like this is to undermine the spectator's confident conviction that fantasy and actuality are clearly demarcated and that these demarcations are discernible. All the other scenes are epistemologically destabilized as a result. This is additionally significant because the film exploits the fact that the spatialized distinction between inside and outside serves a metaphorical function in the culture as a way of distinguishing relative socio-economic positions and psychological conditions. Thus, this instability is metaphorically extended to assumptions about class stability and mental stability.

The destabilizing of the inside/outside binarial is also exploited to establish the implications and consequences of the ubiquity of TV, its presence everywhere in social, domestic, and psychic space. The authority of actuality in Pupkin's world is shown to have been usurped by mediated images, simulacra, and delusional simulations that reframe and re-edit events, which then pass for the actuality they had actually disintegrated in the guise of making it seem more coherent, more meaningful. Thus the mother's offstage, fantasy-dispelling, voice at home, which repeatedly calls Rupert's name, calling him back to himself, is finally replaced by the equally offstage voice of the announcer repeating his name, "Welcome Home..." as if to affirm there had always been a more authentic home to which he had belonged all along. The film constructs TV as an alternative space, a liminal psychic space carrying the same affect as "home", because that is precisely how TV constructs itself. The film demonstrates how TV compensates the isolated individual for the anomie it helps construct by performing a substitute, ersatz version of authentic community. If Pupkin seems at home on TV it is because he has lived in and through TV. It is not only that he has made his home in the image of TV, he seems to have made his home *into* a TV.

One of the strangest exploitations of the metaphorical possibilities of spatial coordinates in the film is the extraordinary shot-sequence in which the camera pans out from a black-and-white, two-dimensional image of a laughing audience to reveal Pupkin addressing them from within a room-size chrome-coloured box. This sequence can be said to formulate in purely cinematic terms the defining conditions of what abnormal psychology designates as "borderline personality disorder" – conditions which are characterized by the profound blurring of distinctions and dissolution of boundaries. If the architecture and camera movement of this sequence is intended to evoke, in abstract terms, the impression of a gigantic television set capacious enough to contain Pupkin's house, then this sequence would also seem to be characterizing television's special relation to these so-called borderline states. The sequence is ultimately enigmatic. There is no clearly pronounced diagnosis; it cannot be ascertained with certitude that Scorsese is indicting TV for producing such states or for inducing them in those who are already predisposed to them. But there is in this sequence the suggestion, however vague, that TV itself constitutes the institutionalization of a borderline condition – that its whole rationale as an industry, as a cultural institution, as a set of practices is to mimic, to construct, and to effect exactly the modes of experience that characterize the borderline personality clinicians designate as narcissistic, in which the sense of a distinguishable and distinct, coherently integrated and bounded, autonomous self is absent.[3]

TV occupies the borderline, *is* the borderline between, De Niro and Scorsese seem to be saying. It mediates between individual subjectivities (each ego's sense that I am I, not you) and the ideal egos that TV celebrities perform for those subjectivities, a set of displayed attributes which when internalized come to constitute their ego-ideal. Celebrity is a multi-levelled system of signs expressing the ideal of achieved individuality: transcendence out of the anonymous mass through strength and uniqueness of personality. The condition of achieved selfhood is the commodity that is marketed by a celebrity such as Jerry Langford. Celebrity constitutes an implicit claim, however bogus, of a self-authored and self-generated, autonomous, integral, coherent, continuity of unique personality. The institution of celebrity has been a means by which consumer capitalism has rationalized and safely organized the irrational needs, desires, and impulses of the crowd. In particular, the TV celebrity provides the illusion of familiarity, intimacy, and immediate access to the celebrity's unique personality and selfhood.

This situation is the basis of the so-called "parasocial" relationship so often reported between spectators and the celebrity personae or characters they see on TV. Such relationships are characterized by a confusion whereby viewers come to think that they are actually in a personal, intimate relationship with someone on TV and tend to react to the vicissitudes of that person's life as if they were those of a friend or family member, or even their own. TV's direct mode of address to an implied "you" (augmented whenever a performer, such as a talk show host, looks directly into the camera), the routinized predictability of programming, the implicit assurance provided by the everyday reliability of the TV celebrity's appearance, the fact that it is

often watched with relaxed psychic defenses or overheard in distraction, and the fact that it is the center of the home all contribute to create the spectator's illusion of familial interactions ("I want to tell you everything about myself," Masha confides).

Television has become a home for many millions of people. It routinely brings the outside world into the domestic sphere and makes its products – the stars and their personae – so familiar as to seem part of the family. Even Langford, whose whole life has been absorbed with TV, seems to have had his life absorbed by it as well: returning to his cold, lonely flat he is greeted only by his trinity of TVs. Here the blurring between within and without becomes for a moment metaphysically eerie as Langford gazes fascinated at the screen's uncanny provision of a movie scene in which a woman is shown taking a handkerchief from a purse while a man looks on. At the level of the plot, this sequence seems to mirror from the independent, almost omniscient perspective of the TV a replaying of the recent exchange of handkerchief between himself and Pupkin; but at the level of discourse, by which the film insinuates implications through the manner of its narration, this sequence seems constructed to call attention to the ubiquitous and strangely authoritative presence of the media and to the activity of addictive gazing which that ubiquity and authoritativeness promote. A somewhat different but related idea about TV is expressed in the sequence in which Langford pauses before a product display window to watch Pupkin perform in his place. When Langford ruefully stares at the mass of mass-produced television monitors, the multiple sameness of their broadcasted image rendering any one of them indistinguishable, the equivalent of a blank screen, it is not just that he recognizes and contemplates with irony and fascination how easily he has been replaced. He is shocked to see Pupkin in a whole new light, the transforming light of TV's aura, which can bestow the halo of public beatification on any *nebbish* that enters its space. This is part of the significance of Scorsese's not allowing the film audience to see Rupert's monologue directly, but only by way of television.

But it is the scenes of Pupkin at home pretending to be on TV interviewing celebrities that most clearly comment on what is most significant about the medium's promotion of quasi-delusional, parasocial, relationships: its blurring of public and private spaces. **King Of Comedy** projects a fantasy of passing through the TV looking-glass to the other side of the screen and occupying a privileged site where the public exhibition of self is not only rewarded but celebrated. This is a fantasy generated first and foremost by the glowing screen itself, beyond any particular image on that screen – by its invitation to passivity and the frustration of the desire to participate that passive viewing dialectically inspires. But Pupkin's fantasy of crossing-over also reflects the medium's own border-crossing, its penetration and occupation of domestic space and its teleportation into the psychic space of the daydreaming spectator of a spectral figure, "Jerry" (the public image and commodified brand name of Langford), who routinely night after night performs the continuity that establishes the semblance of a self. When Pupkin addresses himself to "Jerry" this informality and (delusive) palsy parasociability registers the fact that Langford's meaningfulness for him is as a signifier of having crossed over into the condition of being on a first-name relationship with everyone. Pupkin's "Jerry" is always an address to an achieved "public subjectivity", to a mass-mediated illusion of the achievement of a coherent, inviolable, stable, free agency undetermined by external forces.[4] However, as a signifier of the condition and status of having crossed over (of having been "made" as some of Scorsese's other characters might say), "Jerry" also registers the possession of an envy-inspiring capacity to look back at and to address the anonymous mass of spectators from whom he had extricated himself by virtue of a persuasive claim to uniqueness. De Niro artfully conveys Pupkin's incontrovertible faith in the inevitable recognition of his own deservedness, sometimes subtly, sometimes broadly expressing his character's resolute denial of the possibility of permanent rejection by others, the

possibility of his ultimate worthlessness in their eyes. Pupkin never acknowledges the anger or coldness of Langford or his minions, treating such displays as jokes to be responded to in kind.

Similarly, one of the most alternately pleasurable and excruciating aspects of De Niro's performance of Rupert Pupkin is that he never allows the character to be embarrassed, a defining attribute of many comic agents. Pupkin has courtesy. He is polite to the verge of impudence. But courteous formality of speech is as far as Pupkin can go in abiding by codes and regulations. He has no deep sense of propriety or requisite perspective on what is considered appropriate within the boundaries of particular social spaces, which is the basis for embarrassment. He simply will not know his place. He has no sense of his own inappropriateness in regard to where he positions himself or for how long. He is so little embarrassed that the film audience must be embarrassed for him, even as they also admire and enjoy the *chutzpah* made possible by his obliviousness. This compensatory embarrassment probably derives from partial identification with him. De Niro and Scorsese brilliantly induce anxiety in audience members by compelling them to violate their own sense of propriety by compelling them to partially identify with someone who does not recognize he is out of place and in the way. Yet Pupkin's freedom from self-consciousness is also enviable because it generates his anarchic freedom to get what he wants. His occupation of public spaces therefore becomes a spectacle, fascinating and disquieting by turns because it manifests a profound capacity to ignore and/or an equally profound incapacity to recognize the demarcations between the private and the public, domestic and corporate, self and Other.

It seems evident (the ambiguity of his character demands a degree of hesitancy) that Pupkin has succumbed to television's provision of simulated intimacy. This is why it is possible for him to think of Jerry Langford as his "friend and mentor" even after being jailed. Certainly, Pupkin's most satisfying relationship seems to be with the cardboard cut-out of Langford that he uses as a prop for faking intimacy. But Pupkin might well be faking a laugh of adoration he genuinely feels.

Idealization, as Freud pointed out, is not just the activity of admiring another but the activity of trying to become that Other, a process disastrously facilitated by the narcissistic personality, which cannot distinguish where the boundaries of self ends and that of another begins. The fact that this Other is often a symbolic compensatory substitute for a lost or absent parental figure necessarily promotes crises in which the desire for security through union conflicts with the need to affirm an autonomous identity. The off-stage Langford shows little more pizazz than the cardboard effigy into which Pupkin must pump fake exuberance to achieve even the illusion of his animated presence; but for Masha he is charismatically vivid, extraordinary, a fascinating object of devotion. The fact that the depressively subdued Langford is not charismatic only heightens the irony of Rupert and Masha's attachment to him and their different but similarly confused misrecognition of him as a parental substitute. It is entirely in keeping with such relationships that Langford, in taking the place of the lost or absent parental object of desire and devotion, must also be humiliated and denied in the need to reassert autonomy of self. Thus, he is forced to apologize to his two fans for being stand-offish and "wrong". His humbling reflects the superimposition of an Oedipal dynamic over a transference dynamic. Masha contrasts (and thereby equates) her imagined relationship with Langford with her evidently loveless relation with her parents. Her compulsive need to attach herself to Langford in a dyadic bond that would substitute for the missing security of parental love is correlative with her unstable ego-ideals and her yearning to escape identity completely through an ecstatic dissolution of the boundaries of the self.[5] Her alternation between desiring to be "Black" and desiring to go out of her head (as if everything were a mere lifestyle choice and anyone could be anyone they want to be, just as America's talk-show ideology says) expresses a potentially violent instability. So when she sings "I'm with you always..." it is not so much the fan's erotic promise of dependability and resolve to be loyal that is conveyed, but the implicit threat of the tenacious stalker or fanaticized follower.

Similarly, Pupkin, whose parental relationships are also dysfunctional (on the evidence of his negligible home life and the allegations of his comedy routine), may sincerely idolize Langford; but his behaviour also displays great ambivalence to authority, notably rivalry and aggression towards the regulatory function of the parental superego (Langford's "ground rules" and the corporate "policy" and "standards and practices"). If his monologue can be said to express the rage of the faceless mass of the ignored and unrecognized, just as his emergence out of the crowd articulates its ambitious aspirations, then it can also be said to encapsulate, in Oedipal terms, the aggression common to narcissists against the absent, distant, or weak parental model.

Pupkin's monologue makes explicit comedy's legendary comic aggression, already implicit in the very idea of the "punchline" and in Langford's mock Oedipal strangling *shtick* in Pupkin's daydream of being envied for his comedic timing. His routine expressly articulates comedy as revenge for and redress of childhood trauma fostered by parents. In fact, his appropriation of the public sphere via the confiscation of the talk show host's monologue spot seems intended to allow him to make public spectacle of his own private, parentally-sponsored trauma or perhaps fantasy of trauma (since he speaks of his mother being dead, although the film audience has heard her voice, which then again might be one of his delusions). The occupation of that spot authorizes this public exposure. Pupkin's jokes are not intended by Scorsese to be funny, but they are not without significance at both the level of characterization and at the discursive level of the film's thematic preoccupations. The joke about beating being part of the curriculum is meant to be heard, discursively, as copy-cat, second-hand Jewish victim-comedy. But there are some pointed barbs at commercialized society, whether expressed by Pupkin or Scorsese it is hard to say. The idea that vomiting, rather than smoking, could be interpreted as a "sign of maturity" suggests not just a ridiculous misreading of the social code, but the arbitrariness of all symbolic codifications and the silliness of taking them seriously enough to abide by them. And of course there are the series of jokes about familial and relational dysfunction. The joke about his parents putting down-payments on his childhood exaggerates the depth of penetration of commercial standards into domestic life and serves to define personhood as just another household apparatus, like a TV, as does the joke about being returned by parents to the hospital as defective. At the same time, at the level of characterization, the degradation narrated by Pupkin's monologue functions as a shrewd campaign waged with an awareness of contemporary victim culture. It functions as a strategy of public relations, demonstrating his rise above his circumstantial lot by putting his trauma to helpful use. The monologue shrewdly capitalizes on the contemporary spectator's ideological investment in his or her victim status and in the concomitant ideology of self-esteem and the contemporary ideal of being a survivor. These coded values and ideals must be signalled by anyone striving for TV celebrity and who therefore must establish the illusion of authentic intimacy with their audience. Despite or because of the lame material, Pupkin's overnight success would seem to prove that the more messed up you are the more the masses will love you (as Woody Allen's overnight sensation Zelig observes).

De Niro and Scorsese contrive to ironically implicate their own film audience through their depiction of a TV audience that applauds one of its own for succeeding in crossing the border between private fantasies and public spectacles arranged and mediated by hegemonic institutions which organize those fantasies for profit. When Pupkin triumphantly returns to television from prison, the announcer exhorts the audience to "welcome home... the inspirational..." With this accolade Scorsese is going beyond an easy gibe at the meretricious glamour of transgressors in contemporary cultural life; he is acknowledging here that he knows that however more sophisticated or alert film audiences may be thought to be, he has compelled his film audience to respond to his character in the way audiences are constructed to respond to TV characters and celebrities. His cinematic pastiche of televisual modes simulates TV's pretense of making the unique and extraordinary (i.e., celebrity) part of everybody's everyday. Composed primarily in middle-shot with a reduced depth of field that flattens the image, the film impersonates the negligible depths of TV's surface screen for satirical purposes. Through narrative and cinematic strategies that induce identification, Scorsese gives the audience the illusion of having come to know Rupert intimately as a unique individual. An individual that successfully negotiates the labyrinthine, mediated corridors of power by creatively applying a solipsistic narcissism – the conviction that everything is but a mirror of his own desire – to the rigid structures of corporate bureaucratization – which had promoted his anxiety of being further and further removed from the authentic center of ultimate power and value – in order to fulfil almost literally his desire to "break into show business."

The progress of the life-long *schmuck* Rupert Pupkin toward becoming a probably transitory king of comedy constitutes a satire on the absurd ideological celebration of radical individualism in such a thoroughly mediated world, which reduces individuality to a formula of imitative gestures – the *shtick* of radical autonomy. However admirable or pitiable, Pupkin demonstrates how the radically autonomous self, goaded by an ideology of · individualistic competitiveness, feels no need to answer to and is incapable of aligning itself with social codes, not to say community values. He demonstrates at the same time how, goaded by the ideology of self-definition and lured by the fantasy of self-fulfilment, the narcissistic self shrewdly calculates that the terms of worldly validation dictate modelling its choices, imitatively, on consensus choices and preferences. Thus **King Of Comedy** is also an ironic take on the way celebrities function as "public subjectivities" to represent to the rest of us what individuality entails, what it might be like to be a Self.

Finally, the counter-ideological ending of the film parodies the cherished American idea that you can become what you aspire to. The ideal egos and ego-ideals provided by the media – and no less so those authorized by Scorsese and De Niro – provide their fans not only with emblematic images of how to be in the world but, more fundamentally, with emblematic images of the possibility that one can be at all. This is to say that the ultimate function of the celebrity, that which he or she ultimately commodifies, packages and markets, is the idea, the ideology, of individuality – the idea of the capacity to be an agent, a possessor of a free will capable of transcending deterministic forces and categories operating in the world (such as the boundaries of class). The idea that one can author and authorize one's self. That said, it is all the more ironic that the final shot of the film is not of Pupkin in his glory but of his cardboard cut-out, as if to say, this is the thin condition of celebrity: nothing more than an image, a life-size facsimile, an ad for the ideology of personality.

Just what is "with you always"? Just what is inescapable? The poor may not be with you always, as it once was declared, it depends where the camera is pointed, but certainly: narcissistic pathologies, celebrities, fanatics... and, for the foreseeable future, TV.

NOTES

1. In a formulation that goes far to establish the discursive links between Rupert Pupkin and Travis Bickle, the screenwriter of **King Of Comedy**, Paul Zimmerman has testified, "I saw a... show on autograph hunters, and thought, My God, they're just like assassins... I also read a piece in *Esquire* about a guy who kept a diary of talk-show hosts as though they were his friends." Bickle, of course, is also a lonely confider in diaries. "Paul Zimmerman: Screen-Writing Is Like The Priesthood", *American Film* 8, #2 (November 1982), p.72.

2. There are of course numerous references to the phenomenon of mass-mediated celebrity and its ambiguous fan-base in **Taxi Driver**, the most significant parallel being Bickle's acquisition of newspaper notoriety.

3. Christopher Lasch, among others, has persuasively argued that narcissism and other borderline personality disorders constitute the definitive psychiatric condition of the postmodern epoch, just as hysteria had in the early decades of the 20th Century and schizophrenia did in the decades after World War II. See his *The Culture Of Narcissism: American Life In An Age Of Diminishing Expectations* (New York: W. W. Norton, 1978).

4. The concept of the celebrity's "public subjectivity", which varies somewhat in type and structure from medium to medium, is analyzed by P. David Marshall in *Celebrity And Power: Fame In Contemporary Culture* (Minneapolis: University of Minnesota Press, 1997).

5. Charles Lindholm's survey of theories about the phenomenon of charisma and its psycho-social origins and implications, *Charisma* (Oxford: Blackwell Publishers, 1990), is instructive about the ambivalence driving the narcissistic personality type toward and away from the public figure made to function as a symbolic parental substitute.

ROBERT DE NIRO, THE GANGSTER FILM AND 'ONCE UPON A TIME IN AMERICA'

Once Upon A Time In America (1984) represents a crucial link in the assessment of De Niro's contribution to the gangster genre. Situated between the earlier "star making" roles in **Mean Streets** (1973) and **The Godfather Part II** (1974) and the later, ironically supporting roles in **The Untouchables** (1987) and **Goodfellas** (1990), Noodles Aaronson remains De Niro's most comprehensive interpretation of the gangster figure despite its deviations from our perception of the classic model. It is this very deviation, while still drawing from both generic convention and De Niro's meaning as "star" which marks the role as central to both the contemporary version of the film gangster and the genre star.

The value of association has been crucial to the development of the genre star. Even some of the most rigidly generic or formulaic films have benefited (at least commercially) from the guarantee that a star performer would pursue variations on familiar narrative situations. This can, of course, simultaneously hinder a particular work, imbuing it with the safety (or complacency?) engendered by a star repeatedly enacting a persona in overly common scenarios. Such repetition, contrary to the popular wisdom of both star and studio, may induce a cumulative indifference to seeing *that* star do *that* thing just once too often. Recently, to confirm this, one need only examine the sporadic attempts by both Arnold Schwarzenegger and Sylvester Stallone to shed the iconic (if not the ideological) baggage accrued by the personae they cultivated in several action films produced in Reaganite America. Indeed, there seems to be a pronounced tension between their presumed cultural identity (their value to audiences as film stars) and the types of films they feel they need to make. While the former has achieved modest success with a sequence of "family" oriented films (**Junior** [1994], **Jingle All The Way** [1996], **Batman And Robin** [1997]), the latter saw no option after the critical and commercial failure of **Oscar** (1991) and **Stop Or My Mom Will Shoot** (1992) but to retreat back to the action heroics of **Cliffhanger** (1993), **Demolition Man** (1993) and **Judge Dredd** (1995).

Those stars less readily (or even exclusively) associated with a generic form have nevertheless made contributions which inform crucially not only their own screen personae but the genre as a whole. In this instance, James Stewart's contributions to the Westerns of Anthony Mann would be exemplary, highlighting a growing ambivalence toward the myth of the Western hero while never eclipsing the "Capraesque" notion of the actor's personality. Conversely, a talented character player such as Anthony Perkins spent the rest of his career after **Psycho** (1960) trying to live down a role central to the development of the horror film. Nevertheless, the value of actors to specific genres remains crucial in any overview, regardless of the actual volume of their contribution. James Cagney's seminal status in the ranks of screen gangsters belies the fact that only around a quarter of his roles were in that particular genre. However, the lasting significance of some of Cagney's most familiar gangster roles (**Public Enemy** [1931], **Angels With Dirty Faces** [1938] and **The Roaring Twenties** [1939]) is attributable not only to their place in the formative period of the genre but also to the value placed by Warner Bros in a star's association with specific forms. Any discussion of the gangster genre inevitably invests significant time in the contribution of its key male stars – Cagney, Humphrey Bogart and Edward G. Robinson for example, all being central icons in the "golden age" of the crime film.

Robert De Niro does not fulfil the traditional criteria of the "classic" genre star. While his frequent roles in gangster films have secured his centrality to contemporary perceptions of the gangster figure, he is not burdened by a particularized generic persona. Of course, De Niro's career (and importantly, his active career *choices*) cannot adequately be compared to those genre stars of the studio era in which contractual clauses demanded that most stars, even as their bargaining power increased, often played roles against their wishes. De Niro's career in genre cinema has been sporadic and since the '80s, by which time his star "power" had been fully consolidated, his gangster roles have been a product of conscious choice in which his creative input has been considerate at many levels of production. Strange as it may seem, **Once Upon A Time In America** represents, along with **Casino** (1995), the only film in which De Niro occupies the sole lead role in a gangster film (**Heat** [1995] was very much a double header with Al Pacino). Nevertheless, along with Pacino, no other "major" actor has been so central to the modern revisions (or regressions) of the American gangster film[1]. Indeed, by 1987, such was the value placed in De Niro's generic capital that he was cast as the most famous gangster of them all, Al Capone in Brian De Palma's **The Untouchables**.

By the production of **Once Upon A Time In America**, Robert De Niro had appeared in four films to which we could reasonably attach the label "crime" or "gangster" film: **Bloody Mama** (1970), **The Gang That Couldn't Shoot Straight** (1971), **Mean Streets** and **The Godfather Part II** all featured De Niro in, to varying degrees, supporting roles. However, the latter two in particular have become central to discussion of the genre's development and mark both a return to and departure from, the iconography of the gangster film's acknowledged "golden age". **The Godfather Part II** placed De Niro (as the young Don Vito Corleone) in a historical past which evoked the period oft presented in the films of the 1930s. Conversely, **Mean Streets** was strikingly contemporary, transplanting the genre's familiar theme of redemption on to a more avowedly personal, spiritual canvas and infusing it with a kinetic, stylistic energy heavily influenced by European "art" cinema. Importantly, both films were able to draw from the genre's prevalent structures and themes while remaining faithful to the spirit of risk and experimentation which marked some of the so called "New Hollywood" productions of the 1970s. Moreover, both films draw heavily from an accepted concept of the socio-historical permutations of Italian American masculinity and its dominant familial structures. Placing great emphasis on ensemble performances (despite the nominal lead presence of Harvey Keitel in **Mean Streets** and Al Pacino in **The Godfather Part II**), De Niro's contributions were central to these films while being far from dominant.

Therefore, as a modern variation on the star as genre icon, De Niro's value has been defined by his subservience to the codes and structures of the individual film and its ultimate relationship to the genre as a whole. Indeed, his status within the genre would appear monolithic without being overpowering, either in relation to his star image or the genre in general. Later performances *have* threatened to upset this balance – De Niro's Al Capone in **The Untouchables**, while effectively a caricature, is structured upon a series of actorly "set pieces", the gravity of which often overshadow the bland heroics of Kevin Costner's Elliot Ness. **Goodfellas** on the other hand, while acknowledging the tainted romanticism of the gangster figure, never submits to the cold, banal brutality of De Niro's charismatic Jimmy Conway. His contributions to the early films establish a considerable talent for widely diverse roles within generic parameters, signifying the consolidation and "arrival" of a presence bubbling under for several preceding years (has there ever been a more charged entry into widespread recognition than De Niro's first appearance in **Mean Streets** to the strains of The Rolling Stones' *Jumping Jack Flash*?). Alternately, the later films do not rest upon an easily identifiable, recurring personality. Instead, it seems the prime associative value of De Niro is not with an easily identifiable genre or generic type but with what we might call a mainstream "cinema of quality", an apparent assurance that any work to which he contributes will transcend the constrictions of formula or repetition.

Discussing the importance of stars to genre, Andrew Britton argued that:

"The star in his/her films must always be read as a dramatic presence which is predicated by and which intervenes in, enormously complex and elaborate themes and motifs."[2]

Such a reading can only occur in retrospect however, once a considerable body of work has been established. We cannot "read" an actor without the vocabulary facilitated by repeated exposure to their idiosyncratic inflections, mannerisms across a whole range of genres or narratives. A contemporaneous "reading" of De Niro in **Mean Streets** and **The Godfather Part II** (replete with inevitable comparisons to Brando) differs radically from our retrospective "reading" of De Niro in those films, the noted "method" actor, double Oscar winner and familiar genre presence. Moreover, any discussion of De Niro's contribution to the gangster film is qualified by the distinct diversity of his roles. That is, unlike Cagney, the films do not accommodate a recurring personality (regardless of his status in relation to the law) across a range of narratives. Any aggregated formulation of De Niro's "intervention" in the genre has to be mediated by an account of transformation, digression and departure, compounded by the chronological gap of some 20 years which separates his earliest gangster roles from the more recent (**Casino, Heat**). Furthermore, the performances in **Mean Streets** and **The Godfather Part II** are pivotal not only to the reappropriation of genre motifs in the 1970s but also in forging crucial links in the transition of a new, director-driven American cinema into the commercial arena. That the characters (if not the nuances of performance) are so markedly different is symptomatic of the way De Niro has avoided any rigid, restrictive persona in his evolution as a star performer.

Quentin Tarantino has commented that De Niro's status has been regularly enhanced by his association with particular "prestige" creative collaborators (Bernardo Bertolucci, Michael Cimino, Francis Coppola and, most frequently, Martin Scorsese)[3]. The collaborative nature of De Niro's work has extended to an active role in casting choices and the beneficial effect of ensemble playing has often been overshadowed by the attention lavished upon his more celebrated lead performances. **Once Upon A Time In America** is exemplary in this respect, most crucially through the contrasting performance of James Woods as Max. The melancholic introspection and latent violence of Noodles (De Niro) is countered by the visible, oft unleashed psychosis of Max. Indeed, Woods' characteristically edgy, charismatic performance infuses his scenes with De Niro with a dual energy in which both characters' tendency to hysterical expression is given fragile equilibrium. On several occasions Max is prompted to raise his voice or lash out in anger (to Carol [Tuesday Weld], to Noodles himself) and the physical release of Woods' snarls, ticks and gesticulations are a marked contrast to the stillness and silences of De Niro. Indeed, the film is replete with supporting or cameo appearances which reinforce the overall ensemble dynamic and while he plays in key scenes with performers as diverse as Tuesday Weld, Joe Pesci and Treat Williams he also shares highly effective moments with Larry Rap as Fat Moe in the film's 1968 sequence. The ensemble dynamic extends beyond cast interaction with De Niro, particularly Danny Aiello (with whom he never actually shares the screen) and the group of young actors portraying the adult characters as youths (Scott Tiler, Rusty Jacobs, Jennifer Connelly). Again, this has been a common feature of De Niro's career and he is perhaps one of the least "selfish" of all major screen actors. Just a glance at De Niro's filmography as a lead actor reveals a striking consistency of supporting or co-players. Christopher Walken and John Cazale (**The Deer Hunter** [1978]), Joe Pesci and Cathy Moriarty (**Raging Bull** [1980]), Robert Duvall (**True Confessions** [1981]) and Charles Grodin (**Midnight Run** [1988]) all share screen time with De Niro in which they are allowed to use De Niro as a foil to their own character riffs or improvisations, often utilising clashing performance styles in service of the greater good of the film itself. This collaborative sensibility prompted James Monaco to comment that:

"Considering the range of films he has made with De Palma, Scorsese, and Coppola during the last 15 years, De Niro must be considered as the most influential actor of his generation"[4]

Such influence prompts questions as to just what kind of star image De Niro represents and its value to both the individual film and the collective genre. **Once Upon A Time In America** is particularly curious in this respect. It is the work of a filmmaker renowned for his transformation of the iconography of genre (specifically, the Western) into a dazzling play on surfaces, both establishing and consolidating the iconic value of generic signs and forms. Yet this would seem to be transparently at odds with the internalised method performance style of De Niro. Despite his renowned love affair with Hollywood's golden age, Martin Scorsese's films with De Niro constructed a thorough interrogation of many of the ideological assumptions as they were expressed through genre (for example, the musical [**New York, New York**, 1977], as well as the aforementioned gangster films). Scorsese's use of De Niro enhanced the perception of the star as icon as well as performer. Yet De Niro's iconicity is defined less through ideological or political attachments (as was undoubtedly the case with figures like John Wayne, James Stewart or, more recently Sylvester Stallone) than the meanings generated through his status as *artiste*. Indeed, the moral and ideological ambiguities of **Taxi Driver** (1976), and **The King Of Comedy** (1983) suggest a basis for the star as arbiter of tension and disruption rather than cohesion and unity. Furthermore, De Niro seems to have deliberately tackled these roles in order to address the richness implicit in the outcast, the "nobody". **Once Upon A Time In America** builds upon this notion while providing several extraordinary deviations of its own. Enamoured of the iconographic power of the image

and seemingly reluctant to give the genre a thorough *ideological* overhaul, Leone nevertheless manages to forge a work that perfectly complements the cultural, artistic and ideological inflections of its star. This merging of formal and performance styles prompted Leone to reflect, perhaps reluctantly:

"For better or worse I had [previously] worked actors like marionettes... so for the first time, in this film, I have had to follow an actor's ideas without destroying my own. Yes, Bobby will have his *interpretazione artistica*."[5]

In retrospect, **Once Upon A Time In America** seems both a valedictory and a transitional film. It signposts roughly the end of De Niro's apparent "selectivity" of role choice and the final work of Sergio Leone (after a decade's hiatus). It would be four years before De Niro played another lead (in **Midnight Run** [1988]) opting instead to take a series of cameos and supporting roles after which his appearances became much more prolific. On the other hand, the film also represents De Niro's return to the genre in which he established his star status, and the first attempt of a filmmaker hitherto associated almost exclusively with Westerns. As a "pure" genre experience however, the film represents what Adrian Martin calls "a very curious and attenuated exercise".[6] While the film draws from the multifarious iconography of the "classic" gangster film, there is a fissure between its rich texture of generic signifiers and the means by which it accommodates and expresses the familiar themes and motifs. Furthermore, the film draws substantially on several historical permutations of organized crime (prohibition, unions, the move into "legitimate" enterprise) while never wholly centralising their narrative importance. Rather, the film takes both cinematic and historical conventions of the gangster as given and utilises them as a foundation, interweaving their signifying weight with the foregrounded play on formal and character conventions. Its surface textures provide a virtual index of gangster motifs and signifiers yet while the film is "epic" in both intention and effect, the ultimate narrative drive is much more intimate than spectacular.

Central to the film's romantic address is a concern with the mythic notion of a "lost" America and its prevalent social, sexual and economic structures. This was central to **The Godfather** series, itself avowedly "epic" in its ambitions, and has traditionally provided a foundation for the "rise and fall" narrative of the gangster film. Yet the complex temporal digressions of **Once Upon A Time In America** preclude any such progression – the "fall" of Noodles Aaronson has been established 20 minutes into a film running for the best part of four hours[7]. Despite the transplanting of "art" film sensibilities (a fracturing of time, the highly self-conscious manipulation of *mise-en-scène*) onto a generic surface, the film seems intent on preserving the

gangster film's preoccupation (particularly in its earlier incarnations) of an essentially tragic protagonist within the "epic" structure. Robert Warshow argued that:

"What matters is that the experience of the gangster as an experience of art is universal to 'Americans'. In ways that we do not easily or willingly define, the gangster speaks for us, expressing that part of the American psyche which rejects the qualities and the demands of modern life, which rejects 'Americanism' itself."[8]

The gangster as an "experience of art" seems important here, not only through the shape that the genre has bestowed upon the criminal but more crucially in the way the film subsumes the gangster's *given* meanings into an unfamiliar structure. Warshow suggests that a key facet of the gangster's appeal lies in his *rejection* of "Americanism", of the constricts of civilised modernity. This confrontation with civilisation (or at least the processes of civilisation) has been central to the development of both the Western and gangster hero, defining their essence through myth. While the film is replete with, and seemingly completely aware of, its manipulation of the mythic implications of the gangster hero, **Once Upon A Time In America** is unforthcoming in any sustained critique of such assumptions. Instead it draws quite ambivalently on the genre's prevalent attitude toward the gangster. Historically of course, any apparent celebration of criminality in the genre's "classic" model was negated by a (Hays Code-imposed) narrative clause which repeatedly contrived to punish its gangsters for their transgressions. Warshow bestows the quality of tragedy upon a figure whose social infractions are enacted largely within the confines of an already lawless milieu. While the gangster may reject restrictive social codes of civilized modernity, his socio-economic essence is expressed paradoxically through a bastardisation of capitalism (that is, the accumulation of wealth through organised criminality) consolidated through extortion, intimidation and ultimately, violence.

The crimes of Noodles however, extend beyond the capital-controlled confines of the "organized" criminal sub-structure, encompassing personal drug use and, most disturbingly, rape. In accordance with the societal spread of drug-related crime, the presence of narcotics have become commonplace in the crime film (perhaps finding their ultimate expression in Brian De Palma's remake of **Scarface** [1983]). These additional social transgressions are not merely surplus to the film's embodiment of the gangster figure but infuse it with new layers of signification. The visual jolt of explicit rape and drug-taking is at odds with the film's elegiac tone of romance and loss, a constant reminder of the gulf between Noodles' inescapable "smell of the streets" and the impossibility of his romantic yearning. In short, the film confirms Warshow's thesis while constantly usurping its foundation. Noodles' desire to remain independent from the domineering structures of large-scale criminality mean his small-time ambitions and drives mute our sense of his tragic dimensions. Instead, he chooses to obsess over an unrequited love and a friendship tainted by betrayal. It is Max, his own "rise and fall" fuelled by corruption, who represents the film's truly tragic figure, a tragedy itself diluted by its decentering in the narrative. Noodles, on the other hand, fulfils the childhood condemnation by Deborah that he'll forever remain a "two bit punk". Importantly, unlike a brace of "tragic" gangster figures before him, Noodles does not go down in a hail of gunfire (even Tony Montana in **Scarface**, perhaps the most vicious and venal of all modern film gangsters, was allowed to go down fighting). Instead, he is allowed to grow old, embittered, alone, defeated.

The allusion to fable or fairy tale in the film's title unavoidably conjures the figure of the prince and virginal maiden and Noodles' attempts at assuming the mantle of the former are somehow pathetic in their grandeur (represented most explicitly by his hiring of a magnificent restaurant and orchestra for himself and Deborah). Indeed, through the precision of period detail, the film often draws striking contrasts between its idealised setting and the corrupt figures which inhabit it. Noodles' reaction to Deborah's rejection of his overblown courtship makes explicit the latent psycho-sexual dimension often implicit in the gangster figure. The film clearly articulates the release of misogyny through violence, from verbal humiliation to rape and seems unable to totally extricate itself from the moral confusion and debasement of its protagonist. Therefore, Noodles' rape of Deborah (Elizabeth McGovern) is contrasted problematically with the "rape" of Carol during a diamond heist. The film's conflation of violent and sexual instincts means that the "rape" of Carol (whose invitation to "hit me" is interpreted by Noodles as an incitement to sexual assault) is defined as an extension of active criminality (it makes the heist easier because it "shuts her up") and somehow acceptable because she "asked for it". In contrast, the rape of Deborah can be read as a desperate, perversely romantic gesture in the face of unrequited desire. This is underlined by the fumbling attempts at tenderness (caresses, kisses) in the midst of Noodles' primitive, instinctual act. It is this expression of romantic desperation in the midst of such brutality which empowers the sequence with a hopeless, tragic dimension for both victim and perpetrator.

The film defines misogyny as an extension of the intense homosocial ties which bind the central male group. While several characters comment on Noodles and Max's seeming inability to function independently of each other (exemplified by Deborah's taunt to Noodles over Max's influence – "Go on Noodles, your mother is calling you") their respective maltreatment of women points to a undeclared love – the escalating resentments and mistrust of each other finds expression in the intense verbal or physical abuse of their female lovers. Significantly, the one relationship in which Noodles finds some form of apparent stability (one not defined by violence) is with Eve, a character introduced in the film's very first scene, shot through the breast and left sprawled and inert on a bed over the outline of a figure created by shooting bullet holes into a mattress. From the outset, the film conflates misogyny with the pervasiveness of violence, underscored visually in a brief moment during the initial search for Noodles in an opium den, when a thug caresses a woman's naked breast with the barrel of a pistol.[9]

The homosocial impulses embodied by the central male group are crucially inflected by Noodles' romantic yearning for Deborah (despite his explosions of sexual violence he is the only male character in the film seemingly capable of the romantic gesture, however superficial). Because of the intensity of the film's masculine address, the only way the film seems to be able to accommodate its female characters is to subject them to the prevalent brutality. De Niro's apparent affiliation with highly masculinist

narratives is reflected in a filmography beset with accounts of spiritual, ideological or moral crises for the contemporary male hero figure. Robin Wood argues that the films made with Martin Scorsese are concerned primarily with "the social construction of masculinity and its hideous consequences for both sexes".[10]. The gangster genre, with its central discourses of masculinity, provides an ideal platform for such an interrogation, yet Leone's film betrays a pronounced tension between the embracement of generic conventions of masculinity and any rigorous deconstruction. Adrian Turner's earlier comment that the film provides an "attenuated" experience becomes more crucial here in the sense that the film is prepared to articulate the conventions of the gangster figure to the extremes of sexualising the genre's preoccupation with violence yet it is somewhat reticent to provide a comprehensive critique within the boundaries of that account.

Despite the somewhat unconventional take on the gangster hero, De Niro is privileged with several avowedly generic moments (gun fights, heists, "hits"). Indeed, it is Leone's almost fetishized concentration on what Turner calls "clinches, charged looks and gestures, moments of recognition"[11] that infuses Noodles with a romantic persona at odds with the cold acts of brutality of which he is capable. Consequently the film strikes a precarious balance between Noodles' dual embodiment of sexual monster and gangster hero. The violence embodied by Johnny Boy (fuelled by a paranoid psychosis) and Don Corleone (a vacillating expression of personal vendetta and business necessity) did not encompass the brutalisation of women, and until **Cape Fear**, the recurrent sexual threat embodied by De Niro was never explicitly equated with violence (the brutalisation of Vicky in **Raging Bull** is never conceived in sexual terms).

Turner also argues that:

"In Leone's hands, the classic genres become not only Pop Art friezes of iconographic signs and indices, but also a ritual procession of dramatic or 'scenographic' high points."[12]

In stripping genre to its iconographic and dramatic fundamentals, the film's play on the gangster narrative means that its preoccupation with the mythic foundations of American lawlessness is imbued with a mournful elegy on not only the passing of an era but on the meaning of the classic image of the gangster *in extremis*. Defined significantly by its cinematic interpretation, the prohibition era gangster is meticulously preserved by Leone as he condemns it to a bitter conclusion. Death becomes a recurring motif in relation to Noodles, be it the direct consequence of his chosen profession or the indirectly consequential beating and murder of his closest friends. Strikingly, his physical presence in several individual shots or sequences is ethereal or ghostly. The film's opening sequence introduces Noodles via his absence, in an affectionately placed bedside photograph smashed into fragments by the butt of a pistol. It is as if the film is at once enraptured and repelled by the presence of its protagonist, stressing immediately the inherent contradictions of a figure who, in the words of the young Deborah is "altogether loveable" despite the knowledge that "he'll always be a two bit punk". Thus, De Niro, "the quintessential New York icon"[13] of the cinema in the 1970s, becomes an almost spectral reflection of the dynamic figure he embodied in that decade.

This is emphasised throughout the film – the first occasion on which we see De Niro in the streets and alleys of the urban outdoors, he is framed behind the window of Fat Moe's, against the fluttering, strangely eerie debris of the celebrations marking the end of prohibition. The film slowly builds upon this ethereal aspect of Noodles' character, notably during the frozen moment he stands motionless and bound to a thirty-five-year exile, before a mural celebrating the joys of Coney Island. This is consolidated later as he takes part in a gunfight in a feather cleaning plant, framed amidst an obscuring white haze, the angel of death incarnate.

Yet, despite De Niro's inescapable connection to the city landscape, Noodles is seen at disconcerting odds with his urban surroundings, not least during the moments in 1968 when he observes a game of ball played by denim-clad black youths and as he traverses unsteadily through the New York night brandishing a suitcase filled with the money stolen cruelly away thirty-five years previously. In the context of Max's desire to move beyond the strictures of criminality, Noodles' "smell of the streets" becomes an untenable burden in a criminal economy increasingly bound up in the world of "legitimate" enterprise. Noodles responds to Max's accusation that he'll "carry the smell of the streets for the rest of his life" with the exhortation "I like the stink of the streets, it makes me feel good, I like to smell it and it opens up my lungs. And it gives me a hard-on". This proclamation verbalises the film's conflation of the genre's tradition of the "street punk" and the psycho-sexual. The "streets" (euphemistic of the criminal environment) become one more defining factor in the shaping of Noodles' primitive sexuality. Whether coercive or consensual, all of his sexual encounters occur beyond the domestic confines of the bedroom (on the rooftops as a youth with the soon to be brothel madam, Peggy), during a diamond heist (the "rape" of Carol), or in cars (the rape of Deborah, the encounter with a prostitute in a hearse upon his release from prison). These incidents are one more way of aligning the transgressive acts of the criminal with his sexual instincts, precluding the apparent stability afforded by conventional sexual relationships.

In De Niro's Noodles the nervous energy of Johnny Boy and the measured control of the young Don Corleone give way to a figure condemned to the uncertainty of knowledge, a dawning realisation of a betrayal bound by the mysteries of time. The inevitability of death is defined not so much by the acceptance of Noodles' own demise but by a sustained focus on his proximity to ritualised or symbolic enactments of the killing of both his closest friends and greatest foes. Noodles' first act as an adult in the outside world is to have sex in a hearse and despite its comic tone, the sequence is heavily symbolic in its configuration of the sex and death drives. Conversely, his murder of the gangster waiting to apprehend him at Fat Moe's early in the film, frames Noodles in the classic predatory mode, self-preserving, cunning and instinctive. There is a definite visceral thrill in the visual conceit coined by Leone wherein the pursuer's hat is ripped apart by the impact of an exiting bullet. The resulting thick, spidery ooze of blood and fall-out of shot is replaced by a static, momentary long shot of Noodles, confidently brandishing a pistol and triumphant in his cold, merciless execution. The film consolidates such exhilarating spectacles of death with the melancholy of the aged Noodles witnessing the relocation of a Jewish cemetery, his visit to the new resting place of the other gang members and ultimately, the uncertain fate of Max. Now a successful but disgraced politician living under an assumed identity, Max is tormented by the betrayal of his friend, and his apparent suicide in the back of a garbage truck condemns him literally to that very "smell of the streets" for which he berated Noodles decades previously.

In both **Mean Streets** and **The Godfather Part II** the contrasting identities crafted by De Niro served both Scorsese's and Coppola's critique of the dominant patriarchal drive inherent in the organised criminal social sphere. Essential to these films was the spiritual (and attendant redemptive) meanings associated with the Italian American, Catholic milieu. Leone's film deviates from a common discursive strategy of the contemporary, white gangster film, that of the Italian American crime family or "Mafia". The Jewish identity (and consequent iconography) of the gangsters in Leone's film has no immediate obvious bearing on the film's narrative or thematic structures. Leone himself, in response to the suggestion that the film should use more Jewish actors declared "Jews, Italians, there's no difference"[14] suggestive in itself that the signifying language of genre transcends the ethnic foci of an individual film.

The dual discourses of genre and auteur produce parallel perspectives on De Niro's star persona as it serves simultaneously the recurring motifs and structures of both the filmmaker and the generic form. The ethnic make-up of the character is less a narrative "hook" than the meaning that De Niro's star identity has in relation to those prevalent structures. Yet all the same,

Leone is careful to furnish the film with all manner of detail which serve as reminders of the characters' religious/ethnic foundation. This is most apparent in the 1920s section (in which De Niro does not appear) and ranges from the clothing and physical accoutrements of extras to the various manifestations of the star of David (even in the window of Fat Moe's bar). It is also apparent in isolated speech patterns or phrases between various characters who occasionally greet, toast or curse each other in Yiddish. The tendency to hysteria, manifested by Johnny Boy in **Mean Streets**, seems bound by a critique of a particularized strand of Italian-American masculinity which is sometimes so physically pronounced (the hunched shrug of the shoulders, the outstretched, gesticulating palms, the over-extended greeting of "Heyyyyyyy!") as to unwittingly contribute to the reinforcement of certain ethnic stereotyping. Conversely, Don Corleone, despite his murderous interpretation of capitalism, is defined by self-control and an essentially conservative drive to preserve the structures of "the family". However, De Niro's gangster films have drawn on a much broader range of ethnic identities than is commonly acknowledged (Jimmy Conway is careful to state his Irish identity while Ace Rothstein in **Casino** (1995) is another Jew). Perhaps perversely in a film made by an Italian, its Italian mobsters (Frankie [Joe Pesci] and Joe [Burt Young]) are depicted as the enemy, arrogant, oafish usurpers of the surrogate family headed by Noodles and Max.

Estranged from both the literal and communal family, Noodles' internalised conflict finds its complement in both De Niro's controlled, unmannered performance and the film's fractured, reflective chronology. The so-called "method" approach to acting is readily associated with psychological depth, the "inner" performance. Yet a repeated feature of noted "method" actors is the aspect of *physical* transformation, represented most famously by De Niro and his weight gain for **Raging Bull**. This found its formal correlation in Scorsese's often highly stylized, monochrome visual schemata, and the verbal inarticulation of Jake La Motta was weighed by the film's hyper visual expressiveness. Leone utilized De Niro's method in a very different way, effectively fusing the film's formal structure with the psyche of Noodles. Any physical transformation here is achieved chiefly through make-up and the bodily variation which does occur (such as Noodles' listless, tired walk as an old man) is achieved, in keeping with much of the performance, almost imperceptively. This is combined with the temporal dislocations which formally manifest the "method" conventions of introspection and reflection. While the film draws heavily on De Niro's iconic presence, it benefits as much from silences and stillness as it does from the intense rages of rape and murder. The numerous close-ups emphasizing glances and gestures privilege De Niro's face with a non-verbal expression of the film's central themes. It is wholly fitting that the film's final shot acknowledges the centrality of that face as, photographed from above, it mockingly creases into a grotesque grin and the oblivion of an opium-induced stupor. This final shot effectively obliterates the conscience which has guided our perception of the film's narrative trajectory and its place at the end of the film suggests tantalizingly that the whole narrative has been a drug-fuelled fantasy. While it provides a fitting visual coda to the film's meditation on time and memory, it also locates and cements De Niro firmly in Leone's gallery of iconic visages, a site occupied already by Clint Eastwood, Henry Fonda, Lee Van Cleef and Charles Bronson.

Aside from Dreyer perhaps, no filmmaker has valued the face quite like Leone and its crucial placement in the film's final, frozen image acknowledges the centrality of De Niro's presence in this interpretation of the gangster film. Yet the film does not so much *contain* De Niro as his contribution becomes a fundamental structuring principle. That it can *serve* the film rather than *dominate* it points not only to De Niro's skilfully measured performance but also to Leone's recognition of the possibilities inherent in *interpreting* genre rather than slavishly adhering to its narrative foundations. Furthermore, the film does not so much resemble a compromise of star and auteur rather than a happy collision. If Bobby was granted his *interpretazione artistica* then Leone certainly exercised his. Maybe somewhere in between lies the real essence of this truly elegiac work.

NOTES

1. One could of course add to these names less well known (at least in relative terms) actors such as Fred Williamson, Jim Brown or Pam Grier whose contributions to several crime films of the '70s helped to redefine the gangster figure in racial terms. The dominant tendency however has been to label the films and their stars as representative of "Blaxploitation", thus shifting emphasis from the conventions of genre to the meanings engendered by the admittedly crucial racial discourses. The same could be said of a figure such as Chow Yun Fat in his many crime films produced in Hong Kong – like Cagney again, his screen persona encompasses both cop and criminal (as well as other variations) but the discussion of such films as **The Killer** (1989) or **Hard Boiled** (1991) inevitably centres on their status as action films.

2. Andrew Britton, "Stars And Genre" in *Stardom, Industry Of Desire*, London/New York, Routledge, 1991, p205.

3. Speaking on the Robert De Niro *Cinefile* programme, broadcast on Channel 4, 1994.

4. James Monaco, *American Film Now*, New York, Oxford University Press, 1979, p164.

5. Adrian Martin, *Once Upon A Time In America*, London, BFI, p70.

6. Ibid, p37.

7. Such a "rise and fall" progression was reinstated ironically for the film's severely truncated American release in which Leone's complex time shifts were ruined by a chronological restructuring of the narrative.

8. Robert Warshow, "The Gangster As Tragic Hero" in *The Immediate Experience*, New York, Atheneum, 1979, p130.

9. This shot was cut at the behest of the BBFC for the film's British release.

10. Robin Wood, "Robert De Niro", in Nicholas Thomas (ed), *International Dictionary Of Films And Filmmakers: Actors And Actresses*, Detroit/London, St. James Press, 1992, p284.

11. Turner, op cit, p13.

12. Ibid.

13. Quentin Tarantino, quoted on the *Cinefile* programme, 1994.

14. Leone quoted in Turner, op cit, p31.

HIS SATANIC MASTERY: ROBERT DE NIRO IN 'ANGEL HEART'

"Louis Cyphre... Lucifer... huh. Even your name is a Times star joke"

"Mephistopheles is such a mouthful in Manhattan, Johnny"

Angel Heart, 1987 (director Alan Parker), set in 1955 in Manhattan, New York, and Algiers, a town outside New Orleans, Louisiana, is a modern day film noir/gothic thriller based on William Hjortsberg's novel *Falling Angel*, 1978. Starring Mickey Rourke in the central role of down-at-heel private eye Harold R. Angel, known as Harry Angel, the film offers a colourful and twisting mystery, as both the audience and Angel search for clues to the mysterious identity of Johnny Favorite, a famous crooner who mysteriously vanished after the Second World War. Robert De Niro enters the story as Louis Cyphre, Angel's client who employs him to track down Johnny Favorite on the basis of a broken contract. A cruel cat and mouse game is pursued between the three characters which increasingly takes on nightmare and supernatural overtones, climaxing in Angel's dramatic and horrified recognition that neither he nor the other characters are who he thought they were. Robert De Niro's involvement in this film also adds an air of mystery; the film credits refer to him as a "Special Guest", perhaps owing to his status and unusual position of not being in the starring role. De Niro appears in four scenes in the film; as Lucifer in the guise of a cultured American gentleman, he is the enigmatic game master whose clues Angel must follow. Like the character that he plays, Louis Cyphre, De Niro is a master of the elusive; the usual trappings of stardom, industry gossip and glossy interviews do not exist to elucidate the acting motives of a man who is a perfect acting cipher himself. But perhaps the same can be said for De Niro as for the fictional Louis Cyphre; "If I had cloven hoofs and a pointed tale would you be more convinced?".

    Angel Heart takes the form of a detective story with an unusual and gothic twist in the tale, or as Parker states: "The fusion of two genres, a fantastic Faustian tale told as a classic Raymond Chandler detective story"[1]. Instead of deciphering clues which will allow him to pin down the identity of a criminal, Angel is directed to follow a path of clues laid down by Louis Cyphre which leads to Angel's discovery of the criminal as himself, albeit in the form of Johnny Favorite. Angel effectively has the cipher-key to the mystery all along but fails to recognize this, just as he does not even express recognition or curiosity that Louis Cyphre is word play on Lucifer, and also, on an interpretive level, stands in for cipher. Favorite's story goes as follows: he sells his soul to the Devil in return for stardom, which he achieves with his hit "Girl Of My Dreams". Favorite then attempts to evade his debt by finding an obscure rite in an ancient manuscript. His deception involved eating the warm, still beating heart of the young Harry Angel, a soldier celebrating New Year's Eve in Times Square in 1942. Favorite thereby sacrifices Angel's soul but inhabits his identity. Both souls then inhabit the body of Johnny Favorite but Angel's soul hides Favorite's soul and identity. Favorite is helped in leading Angel to a New York hotel and performing the grotesque ceremony by his New Orleans high society girlfriend and fellow black magic practitioner Margaret Krusemark (Charlotte Rampling), and Toots Sweet (Brownie McGhee) a New Orleans bluesman, and Voodoo worshipper.

Only Favorite knows the identity of the young soldier that he has killed; he takes Harry Angel's dog tags and gives them to Margaret to seal in a vase. Johnny is drafted in 1943 and is badly injured about the head and face in an attack in North Africa, and he is sent home. He is sent to a veteran's hospital in Alderney, upstate New York and registered under his original name, Johnny Liebling. Initially Favorite arrives in a coma and is later diagnosed as being an incurable trauma case suffering from acute amnesia, or in Cyphre's words a "virtual zombie", a "vegetable". Favorite's medical expenses are paid for by Cyphre. Margaret and her father Ethan Krusemark (Stocker Fontelieu) "rescue" Favorite from the hospital and use $25,000 to bribe his doctor, Fowler (Michael Higgins) into recording a false transfer to another hospital. Favorite leaves the hospital in bandages; his face has been extensively damaged in the war and he has undergone extensive facial reconstruction. Margaret and Ethan Krusemark then drop Favorite off in Times Square on New Year's Eve 1943, in the hope that this will allow Johnny to be fully hidden within the re-activated memory of Harry Angel, because the location and occasion could allow Angel to connect with his former life. Harry Angel does connect with his former life without recollection of his encounter with Johnny Favorite. This is the situation that Cyphre must alter; Cyphre needs Harry to recognize himself as Favorite before he can collect the soul that is his due.

Angel Heart opens in heightened film noir fashion, a dark destitute street, steam rising from manhole covers, rubbish littering the street, the yowling of a neighbourhood cat, synthesizer sounds and mournful saxophone music[2]. A dog is seen stopping in front of a bundle which turns out to be a dead body. The film then abruptly cuts to 1955, daytime Brooklyn, with noisy neighbourhood sounds; male operatic singing, busy traffic, and phones ringing. Angel is seen amongst the disarray of his office, he receives a call from the attorney firm of Winesap and Mackintosh who ask him to go to a church in Harlem to meet their client Louis Cyphre. Harry agrees but has difficulty with the client's name asking, "Is your client a foreign gentleman?" Indeed Cyphre's name is the most obvious clue/cipher in the film which the audience picks up on very quickly – but not the unfortunate Angel, who is so lost in piecing together details that the obvious seems to be constantly one step ahead of him. He is unable to translate its symbolic meaning perhaps due to his problems with its pronunciation or because at a deeper level he is unconsciously resisting being able to identify anything – including language which might reveal his true identity as Johnny Favorite. Indeed, the audience plays the real role of detective in the film, whereas Angel is seen as more of a confused victim.

Angel goes to Harlem, entering the church he hears a gospel sermon in full swing; as Pastor John talks to his flock about reincarnation, Angel climbs the stairs to the balcony overlooking the congregation hall and witnesses the hypocrisy that can enter organised religions, as the Pastor demands that his flock make him rich; "I want you to show how much you love God. It's your task... I want you to open up your hearts, and open up your wallets, and open up your pockets and give it up... Praise the Lord... Someone been talking about me. Talking about how I ride around in a Cadillac. If you love me and want to give to me then I should be driving around in a Rolls Royce". Angel is approached by Winesap, a balding spectacled figure in a nondescript overcoat. Winesap leads Angel past a room where a member of Pastor John's flock is cleaning the bloody remains of her husband's brain from the wall against which he shot himself. Winesap leads Angel through a door into a larger reception room with the fading sound of the gospel choir below singing "The word of God, the word of God".

The room is initially silent and the camera focuses on a hand turning a walking stick, which creates a squeaking sound against the floor. The camera cuts to an angled view of a large ceiling fan. Such fans appear constantly throughout the film and function in a similar way to the music by being descriptive, symbolic, and creating repetitive references/clues to Angel's real identity, which the audience picks up on (for example a fan in the window of a room in a large brown brick building is seen three times during the film and refers to the hotel room and ritual whereby Harry Angel was killed by Favorite). Angel is introduced to "Monsieur Louis Cyphre". Cyphre has long white, beautifully manicured, talon-like nails. He wears a large gold ring with an inverted pentacle design on the third finger of his right hand, the pentacle being an occult symbol, and signifier of the Satanic when worn inverted. His hair is dark and long, worn in a greased back bun at the back of his head. He also has a neatly trimmed beard and mustache. He wears an understated smart black suit with a white shirt and black tie. His manner is regal and pious as he sits throne-like in a large chair framed by curtains.

Cyphre remains seated throughout the meeting while the other two stand before him. He is softly and politely spoken. His use of language is a strange mixture of the considered, gentleman-like, archaic and modern day phrases, giving the impression that he is translating his words not so much from a different language but from a different time. Cyphre's use of language has both a surface and a deeper meaning, aware that he is talking to both Angel and also on a much deeper level, the hidden identity of Johnny Favorite. However the guise of "foreign gentleman" is enough to fool Angel, the urbanite Brooklyn dweller – or so he thinks.

Cyphre has an air of command and power which remains under-stated, with a slight air of impatience and irritation which suggests that he is repressing a more volatile and aggressive nature. Cyphre's easy confidence and power gently undermine his role of needy client. He also has a genial sense of fun which is sinister in its tendency to linger for longer than is necessary. It is as if Cyphre has a private joke which he expects Angel to know and is both annoyed and patronizing in reaction to the detectives's ignorance. Cyphre is rather like a lion-tamer, who having taught his lion to do a trick, finds that the lion is unresponsive – so he must wear a fake smile, coax the lion, and appear as at-one with his animal to the audience, when he thinks that the lion might be being deliberately unresponsive and would probably prefer to whip it, but would risk losing both the lion's and audience's willing participation. Yet unlike the lion-tamer, Cyphre is also enjoying himself because he knows that Angel will eventually perform whether he wants to or not. Cyphre has to play a waiting game without revealing to Angel his true nature, which would scare Angel away from his quest to find Johnny Favorite. Cyphre is slightly slimy in his gently persuasive manner – he has to be manipulative to out-manipulate Johnny Favorite from his hiding place beneath the identity of Harry Angel.

The audience are in the strange position of being slightly conspiratorial with Cyphre by virtue of his appearance, which creates the sense that this genial man is being false in his need for help from Angel. Cyphre is obviously hiding something, and in this respect the audience can identify with Angel's sense of unease and curiosity, yet unlike Angel most audiences recognize pentagrams and men with long claw-like nails as being something other than "foreign". Harry obviously feels out of his depth with a person like Cyphre but is unable to pin down his unease or feel in control of the relationship. His attempts to penetrate Cyphre's character and motives are merely swept away.

Cyphre grins at Angel and submissively questions him; "I don't want to appear rude, impolite, but do you have any ID, stuff like that before we begin? It's nothing personal it's just that I'm a little over-cautious, you know how these things are". Angel takes out his ID and hands it to Cyphre, who holds out his hands in a gentle Christ-like gesture of benediction to receive the document. Angel tries to assert his presence telling Cyphre and Winesap that he doesn't get involved with work that is too heavy. Harry asks, "How did you hear about me? I guess you guys just looked in the phone book?" Cyphre shakes his head slowly and heavily with gravity, the left side of his face is hidden in shadow. He does not enlighten Angel with an answer; he is visibly annoyed because he knows Angel's real identity and doesn't like wasting time and being treated like a fool, even if Angel is unaware of his true nature.

Cyphre tells Angel about Favorite, gently prodding Angel to test his self-recognition as Favorite; "Do you by any chance remember the name Johnny Favorite? A crooner before the War, quite famous in his way?". Angel replies in the negative. Cyphre prods, "You never knew him?" Angel interrupts Cyphre's narrative, "Mister Cyphier..."; Cyphre corrects his pronunciation, but Angel still gets it wrong; "I'm sorry baby, I'm sorry Mister Ciphers". Cyphre refuses to be deflected; perhaps sensing that Angel is being deliberately uncooperative, he continues, "His real name was Johnny Liebling...". Cyphre tells Angel that Favorite was drafted into the special entertainment services during the War but returned home a "virtual zombie", and that his contract with Favorite had stated that "certain collateral was involved to be forfeited in the event of his death". Angel expresses empathy with Favorite's patriotic injury, Cyphre quietly exclaims, "Why? Were you in the services Mister Angel?". Cyphre then quietly states his motive for tracking down Favorite, "You know how these things are – he remained a vegetable and my contract was never honoured... I don't want to sound mercenary or anything, but you must understand that my interest in Johnny is only in finding out of he's alive or if he's dead".

At the mention of Favorite's possible death Cyphre proceeds to give Angel a wide Cheshire Cat grin and exchanges conspiratorial glances with the sycophantic Winesap. Angel asks Cyphre, "You want me check it out?" Cyphre replies in the affirmative but in a cheery and nonchalant way as if the deed has already been accomplished. Still in mirthful mood Cyphre plays with Angel a little more, like a cat who has a mouse by its tail; "It's funny, I have a feeling I've met you before". Cyphre is like a sinister clown who gets his perverse pleasures from bullying children. Angel and Cyphre shake hands; Angel replies, "No I don't think so". Cyphre laughs at Angel's reply, but has no intention of sharing the joke.

Angel then travels to the Sarah Dodds Harvest Festival Memorial Clinic in Poughkeepsie, upstate New York, his conversation with Cyphre ringing in his ears. Inside the home Angel pulls out his wallet and flicks through various fake ID cards including a press card, and a US Customs Agent card. He puts on glasses and introduces himself to the receptionist; "My name is Henry

Conley and I'm with the National Institute of Health". Angel says he's researching "incurable trauma cases" and is particularly interested in "Jonathan Liebling". He manages to sweet talk the receptionist into showing him the attendance records, which state that Favorite was removed and transferred to another hospital on New Years Eve, 1943. Favorite looks at the authorisation by Favorite's physician, Dr. Fowler, and discovers that the entry must have been added later, because it was written in ball-point pen – which was not invented until much later.

Angel tracks down the morphine-addicted Dr. Fowler who is unable to give him any information beyond the fact that Favorite was collected by a well-dressed southern gentleman and a woman who waited in the car (the Krusemark father and daughter team). The doctor says that he "truly can't remember" any further details. Angel locks the addict in his bedroom and leaves him to go cold turkey in the hope of gaining more information later. However, on his return, Angel discovers that Fowler has shot himself in the head with bullets taken from the false pages of a hollowed-out Bible. Once again the camerawork lays emphasis on a fan in the room. The room was still locked when Angel entered the room, and only Angel had a key.

To the sound of an opera record, Angel enters an Italian restaurant to meet his sinister client once more. The restaurant is large and very clean. Cyphre is the only customer. The camera focuses in on the table where a tall dish can be seen holding three immaculate white, hardboiled eggs – a gastronomic Holy Trinity. Cyphre is terse with Angel, asking him why he did not see Favorite. Angel is not impressed by the mysterious nature of his quest, which is beginning to leave a trail of death; it's out of the league of a small-time private-eye. Cyphre tries to bribe him; "If the fees bother you we can have them adjusted". Angel replies, "Mr. Cyphre, *you* bother me". Cyphre then says: "I'll instruct my lawyer immediately to send you a cheque for five thousand dollars, if you don't want the job I'll find somebody else". Cyphre then picks up one of the eggs and holds it in both hands between his long nails. He looks down at the egg and slowly begins to peel it, saying, "It looks like our Johnny has found himself a perfect disappearing act". He then cracks the egg on the table, adding, "Well you know what they say about slugs?" Angel; "No, what do they say about slugs?". Cyphre cracks his egg again and replies, "They always leave slime in their tracks". He then cracks the egg loudly and rolls it across his plate under his outstretched hand towards Johnny and back again. With his head tilted, Cyphre looks intensely at Angel and says, "You'll find him". Angel then begins to talk about Fowler whilst Cyphre peels his egg, adding "Did you kill him?... mmm", raising his eyebrows in savoured pleasure at the idea of murder. He then rolls the egg and grins at Angel, asking "Are you afraid?" Cyphre continues with peeling his egg slowly like an orange, letting the shell drop onto the table. Angel says, "You must want this Johnny pretty bad huh?". Cyphre gives Angel another intense look and, letting a large strip of shell fall abruptly to the table like a lead weight, Cyphre replies, "I don't like messy accounts".

Cyphre, with Angel firmly on the case once more, returns to his deeper motive, more aimed at Favorite than at Angel. He states: "You know some religions think that the egg is the symbol of the soul. Did you know that?" He puts salt on the egg and blows it, asking Angel, "Would you like an egg?" Angel replies, "No thank you, I got a thing about chickens", and proceeds to throw salt over his shoulder (a superstitious action relating to warding off occult forces). The camera zooms in on Cyphre's face, and in pure animalistic fashion he opens his mouth wide, wrinkling his nose like a wolf snarling, and bites off a large chunk of the egg, reaching out to the egg with his front teeth. Cyphre then chews the egg in bloated gulps at the front of his mouth, producing loud slurping noises. Angel looks on fixated by fear and disgust. Angel is a man of action who would crack an egg with a hammer to obtain information – Cyphre has a more subtle and cruel way of reaching his target, toying with his victim gently and then moving in for the kill.

Angel returns to the church in Harlem and finds a Satanic/Voodoo altar in a small room behind the one where he had first met Cyphre. Below in the congregation hall he is drawn towards a woman seated with her back to him dressed in black, to the accompaniment of his own heart beats; but is attacked when he approaches her. The scene has a nightmare atmosphere. He escapes from his pursuers, and knocks Pastor John from his carrying "throne" during a church street parade. Angel later turns up at a bar where he meets his noir-style blonde girlfriend, a researcher for the *Times* newspaper, who fills him in on some of Favorite's biographic details. Favorite used to play with the "Spider Simpson Orchestra". The band leader Spider currently lives in the Lincoln Presbyterian Home for the Elderly on 138th Street, Harlem. Margaret Krusemark's father owns a large portion of Louisiana. Margaret was engaged to Johnny until he apparently ditched her; she was known as the "Witch of Wellesley". Amongst the information is a photo of Favorite with Blues guitarist Toots Sweet, who was last known to reside in Albany, New Orleans. At this point in the narrative Angel experiences the first of three flashbacks to New Year's Eve in Times Square in 1943, and sees an arm reaching out to tap a soldier on the back, accompanied once again to the sound of heartbeats. He also sees what appears to be a nunnery with two nuns seated and robed in black.

Angel visits Spider Simpson (Charles Gordone), who tells him more about Favorite. Angel later records this bibliographic information onto tape, making reference to Favorite's secret love, Evangeline Proudfoot, who kept "some kind of spooky store in Harlem called Mamma Carter's". Angel decides to wipe this information from the tape; "You don't need to know that Cyphre – I think, uh, secret love should remain secret". Favorite also used to hang around with a certain Madame Zora who had a palm reading kiosk in Coney Island. Angel visits Coney Island, and, wearing a pair of dark glasses with nose visor, he discovers from Izzy, a friend of the palm reader that Madame Zora was none other than Margaret Krusemark, a "debutante... messing around with more than tea leaves", who had returned South. Angel then decides to follow the trail to Louisiana.

Angel visits the French Quarter of New Orleans and conveniently discovers two posters, one of which advertises a future performance by Toots Sweet, the other advertising Margaret Krusemark's psychic services. Angel catches sight of Margaret Krusemark in the street; she gets on a tram and sits in the back half reserved for the "colored" population (segregation was observed legally in 1955). Angel also boards the tram. Margaret looks as if she senses his/Favorite's presence; Angel follows her back to her house and later visits after having made an appointment. Angel gives her Favorite's date of birth as his own, Valentine's Day 1918. Margaret informs him that she also knew someone with the same birth date but says "I don't think you'd like his chart". Angel then admits that he was lying and wants information about Favorite, "It's Johnny's future that I'm interested in". Margaret replies, "He's dead Mr. Angel, and if he isn't he is dead to me". Angel suggests that Favorite must have hurt her very badly; she responds, "We all have our sins Mr. Angel. Lies and cruelty come very easily to some people". Angel notices that Margaret wears a necklace with an inverted pentagram design. Angel makes a pass at Margaret, as if to seduce her; she looks at his palm and tells him, "I don't think you'd like what I see".

While walking through the city Angel comes across a sign for Mammy Carter's Herb Store. An old man and woman are running the store. Angel asks them about Evangeline Proudfoot. The couple inform him that the name of the shop is generic for stores which sell Voodoo herbs, however the woman knew an Evangeline, who had lived in New York and then returned South, but soon died and was buried in Holy Shelter Swamp, Amityville. Angel buys some St John the Conqueror's Root – which, in occult superstition, acts as a ward against witches[3]. Angel visits the small rural settlement of Holy Swamp and sees her grave, 1918–1947. He also sees decayed offerings of food on the grave, and then sees a young woman with her toddler son replacing the offering with fresh food. Angel discovers that this is Epiphany Proudfoot (Lisa Bonet), Evangeline's seventeen year old daughter, and manages to terrify her son with his mask-like sunglasses. Angel is upset by all of the chickens running around the yard. He asks Epiphany about Favorite but she won't give him much beyond, "My mamma had a lot of guys, she liked men". Epiphany then asks "Hey, what are you after him

for, Johnny Favorite?". The phrasing of the question is subtle in its implications, because it actually works as a direct question to Johnny Favorite rather than as a question to Angel *about* Favorite; thus at this point the film slowly begins to merge the two male identities.

Angel's next stop is a Blues bar in town where Toots Sweet is playing. Angel poses as a journalist writing a book on the Spider Simpson Orchestra, and asks Toots about Favorite. Toots is less than helpful about Angel's line of questioning; "He made a record of one of my songs, but that don't make us buddies". He persists, following Toots into the lavatories after his set. Toots is abrupt and then scared after he sees a chicken's claw next to the basin. Angel picks up the claw and questions Toots, but is grabbed from behind by a large bouncer who holds the claw against Angel's face, Angel protests, "Please, I've got this thing about chickens". Angel is thrown out of the club but waits in hiding for Toots. Angel follows Toots to a Voodoo ceremony in the countryside.

Epiphany is seen in a frenzied dance holding a white chicken whose neck she slits, allowing the blood to pour over her white dress and semi-naked body. Toots plays the maracas at this event. It climaxes with Epiphany writhing on the floor on top of a young man. Toots leaves and returns to his hotel room. Angel again follows; once again the *mise-en-scène* echoes film noir, with shots of a fan and a long dark hallway. Toots attacks Angel with a razor-blade, the two men fight, smashing a wall statue of an angel to the ground. Angel then holds Toots down with the razor-blade against his throat and questions him about Epiphany's "hot shoe number with the chicken... I ain't up on all this Voodoo shit, I'm from Brooklyn". Toots quips, "We ain't all Baptists down here son". He tells Angel that Epiphany's a "Mambo priestess like her momma, has been since she's thirteen". Angel says, "As far as I'm concerned any dead chicken's a good chicken"[4]. Toots tells Angel that he hasn't seen Favorite since before the war. Angel is not happy with this reply and stuffs a piece of paper into Toots mouth with his address, in case Toots "remembers" something later. Angel notices that Toots has a gold tooth with the engraving of an inverted pentagram but gets no further information from him. Angel throws down the clean razor-knife on his way down the stairs.

Angel then enters a nightmare territory. He sees the woman seated with her back to him in black, again in what seems to a warehouse space; he sees the razor-blade on the floor and picks it up, but this time it is coated in blood. Angel looks down and sees that his shirt is drenched with blood, he once again reaches towards the woman with his hand but wakes abruptly to discover two police detectives in his hotel room.

The larger, fat detective hands him the note that he had stuffed in Toots mouth. Toots has been discovered asphyxiated. Chocked by his own dismembered genitalia, his apartment soaked in blood. Angel refuses to give the detectives the name of his client, Cyphre, but refers them to Winesap.

Angel goes to a bar and phones Margaret Krusemark. He checks his appearance in the mirror and has another flashback to New Year's Eve 1943; he sees the window fan in the tenement block, and then sees the soldier being tapped on the shoulder. The soldier begins to turn, then a scream is heard, Angel jumps and is brought back to reality by a musician in the bar tapping him on the shoulder. He goes to Margaret Krusemark's apartment, where he finds her dead on the floor. Her heart has been cut out with a long curved blade – which he had examined during his first visit. Angel opens a box on the bureau and finds a desiccated claw-like hand, heartbeats are heard on the soundtrack. Angel rushes to cover his tracks, attempting to avoid becoming a suspect in another murder. He tears out his appointment in her diary and wipes his fingerprints from the room.

Angel then gets in his car and heads for the countryside. Passing by a river baptism he finds himself being followed by a red truck with two men in it. Angel stops the car and walks over a footbridge to a river quay where the two men set their dog on him; they warn Angel: "Margaret Krusemark's old man wants you on the first train home". Angel goes to visit Epiphany.

She tells him that her Voodoo religion is more humane than Christianity, and that Toots was sent the chicken foot merely to get him to keep quiet about Favorite, he wasn't set up or killed for it though. She also reveals that Favorite was her father. Angel returns to his hotel where he receives a message to meet Cyphre in a local white, formal church.

Cyphre is seated halfway down the aisle on a wooden pew, waiting. He addresses Angel in a polite and respectful manner; "I'm so glad you could come... I have a speaking engagement in Baton Rouge and thought it would be an opportune time to catch up on your progress". Angel is in a dishevelled, nervous state, he tells Cyphre that he is upset by the "stiffs" he seems to be leaving in his trail. Cyphre looks at Angel quizzically as if he does not understand 1950's terminology; "Stiffs?". Angel translates; "Dead bodies Mr. Cyphre. Murders". Cyphre responds, "Murders, mmm," again savouring the concept of violent death; Cyphre seems to be enjoying himself. Angel tells him that he has found nothing about the murders, he describes the death of Toots, "this old Voodoo guy Toots Sweet he got choked with a part of the body meant for pissing with".

Cyphre hold up his hand genially warning Angel to stop, he places his hand to his mouth, and makes a gentle pointing gesture, and like a pious Mother Superior says quietly, "This is a church Mr. Angel". Angel replies, "I'll tell you something, I know it's a church but there's a lot of religion going around with this thing. It's very weird and I don't understand it. It's ugly". Cyphre states: "They say there's just enough religion in this world to make men hate each other, but not enough to make them love". Angel is less calm: "I'll tell you something Mr. Cyphre, there wasn't much love around for Johnny Favorite... I think I was bad luck and it's starting to rub off on me. I'm a murder suspect in three cases". Cypher replies quietly and coldly, "I know, Winesap told me. You must be careful Mr. Angel". This is the second time that an ambiguous reference – "I think *I* was bad luck" – is made to Favorite that could include Angel, this time Angel says it himself as if the truth of his identity is rising into his consciousness.

Angel becomes agitated by Cyphre's calm exterior; he questions him about Margaret Krusemark, demanding a direct answer, "Mr. Cyphre, did you know her or not?". Cyphre replies, "I knew *about* her, but I never actually knew her". Angel colourfully describes Margaret's death being like "someone got to her and took out their own Valentine's card". He dryly quips, "I guess she couldn't tell the future for herself". Cyphre responds with equal dryness, "The future isn't what it used to be Mr. Angel – and your conclusions?" Angel replies that Favorite is out there murdering everyone he used to know, and he is being set up for the homicides. Angel is scared, he asks Cyphre, "Why don't you level with me. What the fuck is going on here?" Cyphre replies quietly, "Just Johnny Favorite and the debt that's sold to me Mr.

Angel. I have old fashioned ideas about honour: An eye for an eye... You know, things like that". Cyphre's reply is calm, the tone is civilized and almost dismissive, although the content has violent undertones.

Angel is not convinced by the reply, something is not quite right. He turns on Cyphre, "Who the fuck are you Cyphre?" Cyphre leans forward almost mischievously, "Watch your language". Angel is getting to the end of his tether, "Hey, hey. I don't give a fuck if this is a church. Churches give me the creeps. I don't like churches". Cyphre takes a casual interest which breaks the tension, "Are you an atheist?". Angel replies, "Yes I am. I'm from Brooklyn". The humorous reply breaks the icy atmosphere and Cyphre gets up to leave; he offers Angel more money and tells the detective that he will be in town for a couple more days. Angel, still in a nervous state, refuses the extra money and makes an attempt to calm himself, "If I'm not careful, that five thousand bucks you just gave me could buy me a seat in the electric chair". Cyphre who is standing above him, looks down and gently pats him on the arm twice and leaves the church, to the sound of his cane tapping on the flagstones. Cyphre's gesture might appear almost paternal if his face and eyes were not hidden in shadow.

Angel returns to his hotel in a rainstorm, finding Epiphany asleep in his doorway. Epiphany says that her mother had told her that "Johnny Favorite was as close to true evil as she ever wanted to come", Evangeline was dedicated to Johnny, who was also "a terrific lover". The scene is erotically charged and they have violent sex. Angel has another flashback, this time seeing the tenement window fan from the inside with blood covering the walls. Inside Angel's hotel room the dripping rainwater turns to blood and saturates him and Epiphany, Epiphany screams and the blood disappears. Angel has his third flashback to the events of New Year, the soldier's face is just turning when Angel starts to strangle Epiphany. He is startled and shocked to find himself in the act of strangling the girl. He walks to the mirror, looks at himself and smashes the glass.

A knock at the door heralds the arrival of the two police detectives, the fat one observes Epiphany from the doorway, "Down here Angel, we don't mix with the jigaboos. The colored folk keep to themselves". He has come to question Angel about Margaret Krusemark, "That nigger guitar player of yours don't matter a shit. He was into Voodoo, they eighty-six each other two a week. This Krusemark dame, she comes from a Louisiana money family. White money". The police have not been able to get any information from Winesap and they're losing patience, "This ain't jigaboo town asswipe. You play jump rope with Louisiana Law and I'm gonna stuff your big city smarts right up your New York ass". The fat detective then adds with sarcasm, "Sorry if I made a mess, maybe you can get your nigger to clear it up".

Angel enters his hotel room and finds Epiphany singing Johnny Favorite's hit in the bath, "You are so sweet, if I could just hold your charms again in my arms. Life could be complete". Angel looks at himself in the cracked mirror. He then leaves the hotel and is attacked by Krusemark's men. He escapes, and decides to pay Ethan Krusemark a visit at the local horse race track. Ethan is initially cagey, "As far as I know that dance band scum bag is dead". Ethan admits to his involvement and begins to express great admiration for Favorite, but thought he had vanished from the scene altogether after they had "dropped him off in the crowd and he walked out of our life forever – or so we thought".

Angel becomes increasingly agitated as Krusemark relishes Favorite's plan to out wit the "Prince of Darkness". He tells Johnny about the desiccated hand found in Margaret's apartment, the "Hand of Glory. It's supposed to be able to open any lock". The hand supposedly is that of a murderer, and the hand was cut off while he was still in the noose. Ethan tells Angel about the "unknown" soldier; Angel has a fourth flashback to the soldier being tapped on the shoulder from behind. Angel vomits at the description of the soldier's murder; Margaret was responsible for handing Favorite the dagger. Angel demands to know who the boy was, but Ethan doesn't know, the key lies in the soldier's dog tags sealed in a vase in Margaret's apartment. Angel stares at himself in the mirror, he hears Ethan's voice, "maybe he gained possession of the boy's soul, but he still looked like Johnny to me". Angel stares into the mirror again and leaves in a distressed state.

Returning to Margaret Krusemark's apartment, Angel finds the dog tags of "Johnny Harold Angel"; he screams. Meanwhile the camera cuts to a shot of Cyphre's right hand holding a more macabre cane than on previous occasions – the hand also appears more gnarled and claw-like. Cyphre once again looks as if he's seated on a throne, but this time his hair hangs loose on his shoulders in a Christ-like parody. Angel, still unaware of Cyphre's presence, repeats in a cracked and hysterical voice, "I know who I am". Cyphre's face is passive, he calmly interrupts Angel's anguish with a weary, coaxing voice, "Alas how terrible is wisdom, when it brings no profit to the wise, Johnny". Angel looks at Cyphre and his thoughts can be seen slowly and mechanically falling into place, as he attempts to stand up to Cyphre; "Louis Cyphre. Lucifer... huh. Even your name is a *Times* star joke". Cyphre retorts smugly and dryly, "Mephistopheles is such a mouthful in Manhattan, Johnny".

Angel accuses Cyphre as "posing as the Devil", and guilty of the murders. He still refuses to believe that Cyphre *is* the Devil, and that he is Favorite. Cyphre is angry, he needs Angel to recognize his true identity in order to collect his debt. Cyphre snaps, "If I had cloven hoofs and a pointed tail would you be more convinced?" Angel protests that he wasn't responsible for the murders; Cyphre gleefully grins, telling Angel, "They were all killed by your own hand – guided by me, naturally". Cyphre has come to collect, he tells Angel, "for twelve years you've been living on borrowed time and on another man's memories". Angel walks over to a mirror, Cyphre continues, "What gives human life it's worth anyway, because someone loves it? Hates it? The flesh is weak Johnny, only the soul is immortal...". At this point Angel looks away from the mirror and the camera cuts to Cyphre's face, his eyes turn yellow as he points accusingly at Angel, continuing, "...and yours is mine". The gesture is more passionate than Cyphre's normal behaviour, but the contrast loses some of the sinister atmosphere of the earlier scenes and becomes more like a cheap thrill scene from a horror movie than a spine-chilling revelation.

Angel tries to hold onto denial, "I know who I am". Cyphre, calm once more, taunts him, "Go on Johnny. Take a look. However cleverly you sneak up on a mirror your reflection always looks you in the eye". Cyphre puts on Favorite's record, and Angel has flashbacks to all the murders that Favorite has committed. However, he still repeats his refrain, "I know who I am". Angel returns to his hotel room to find the two police detectives; Epiphany's corpse lays on the bed, she has been killed by being shot in the vagina. Angel tells the men, "She's my daughter", finally recognising that he *is* Favorite. The thinner detective brings in Epiphany's child. The detectives tell him, "You're gonna burn for this Angel". Angel, stunned, replies "I know, in Hell". Epiphany's son points at Angel, and his eyes flash yellow in emulation of Cyphre's eyes in the previous scene. The film ends in noir-style shadow, with Angel going down, down, down, in a caged lift, symbolic of his journey to Hell.

Angel Heart received poor reviews on its release and did badly at the box office, although it has become a popular video release, with growing "cult" film status[5]. In general most reviews of the time refer to Alan Parker's tendency towards stylistic excess. However, they tend to agree that the film is both entertaining and thrilling in its fast pace that keeps the viewer guessing as to what kind of grisly act or revelation lies in store for Harry Angel. The reviewer Roger Ebert, wrote in the *Chicago Sun-Times*: "The movie is by Alan Parker, a director who has vowed to work in every genre. After **Angel Heart**, he can cross two off his list: private eye movies and supernatural horror films. Parker's films are always made with great gusto, as if he were in up to his elbows and taking no hostages; look for example at **Midnight Express, Fame** and **Pink Floyd – The Wall**"[6]. Ebert adds, "**Angel Heart** is a thriller and a horror movie, but most of all it's an exuberant exercise in style, which Parker and his actors have fun taking to the limit". For

Ebert, **Angel Heart** differs from other private eye movies by virtue of its "sly sense of humor, good acting and directing, and a sudden descent into the supernatural". Parker's vision for the film achieved its aim despite an industry-enforced edit of ten seconds from the blood-drenched sex scene between Angel and Epiphany, in order to achieve the MPAA ratings board "R" certificate.

Parker's film differs from the book, creating a more colourful portrayal of events, and also altering the central position of Harry Angel, from victim to maverick killer. Detective fiction functions on two levels; an ordered surface meaning where the detective reads clues which seen in retrospect to lead to the criminal, and a disordered deeper meaning where the criminal is able to function because the relationship between the clue and the criminal is not fixed. In other words, the solution to the mystery appears obvious in retrospect because all other possible explanations have been removed. Detective fiction offers a double act of concealment, it is "based on a *double system of meanings* – superficial and deep: the first is both the manifestation and the cover of the second"[7].

For example, on a surface level the key to the mystery of Angel's identity lies with Cyphre, ostensibly Margaret Krusemark's occult tool; the "Hand of Glory", which unlocks any door, leads to a supernatural solution to the mystery. In the film, Angel is seen to be the holder of literal keys, such as the one to Dr. Fowler's apartment. Both this supernatural and literal use of keys conceal the fact that the key to the mystery lies with Cyphre, and the ability to pin down and understand the significance of his name. A significance has to be translated into modern day usage as Cipher to be fully recognized. The key to the crime is the fact that names/identities cannot be fixed, they are empty ciphers which define nothing until given retrospective meaning. Hence the criminal in **Angel Heart** can not be identified as he flits from Liebling, to Favorite, and Angel, until the soldier's name tags identify him, and Cyphre is identified as the Devil.

This explains why Detective fiction is littered, like **Angel Heart**, with characters who are stereotypes, because guilt is associated with someone who stands out from the crowd and can be traced. Only the criminal is seen as an individual, as someone who does not fit into the order of society. The criminal is someone whose identity appears to constantly slip and must be fixed, so that he/she can be named and defined as a criminal. Detective fiction seeks to place closure on this slippage of identity, by associating clues with a particular individual, a single identity. The construction of clues which lead to the criminal's downfall are a cover-up for the fact that the world is not an ordered place. It is a place where disorder continuously erupts to the surface only to be explained away when society can label the cause.

In this respect Detective fiction is an essentially conservative genre. It protects the status quo by falsely representing whatever may threaten that disorder as being outside of society, but in doing so it also reveals a deeper level of real threat that it must then desperately seek to conceal. If it fails to conceal this contrived cover-up then the ending is not convincing. The detective is also implicated with the criminal, that is how he/she recognizes criminal. The detective uncovers the disorder that underlies social reality, gives it meaning and covers his tracks. The detective's participation in the criminal's guilt is avoided by presenting the detective as a social eccentric/outsider who works alone. **Angel Heart** shows the detective to be the criminal, and thus by association, society as a whole. However this radical conclusion is neutralized by the supernatural, something that lies outside of our rational society. Also Harry Angel is a less than competent detective, he fails to recognize Cyphre's true identity, and only discovers the key to the mystery of Johnny Favorite by being directed by Cyphre.

Hjortsberg's novel shows both Angel and his relationship with Cyphre in a different light. In the book Angel is less of an insensitive character. Cyphre appears to be responsible for the murders, rather than as acting as a guiding hand. The possible supernatural solution of the book, and the victim status of Angel implies that humanity can do little to fix, order and identify the world around it. After all, recourse to the supernatural comes from periods where humanity lacks the ability to understand disorder in its environment. Cyphre's character is also different, he is less aloof and esoteric, more of an everyday cigar-smoking bully than a seductive Satanic manipulator. The film portrays Cyphre as a more Satanic character than in the book. The book does not include Cyphre's "egg is the soul" speech and demonstration, makes no reference to Cyphre's claw-like nails, and does not describe Cyphre's eyes turning yellow in demonic zeal.

However the book's version of Cyphre is more sinister in its conclusion; it removes him from the clearly supernatural because it implies that his devilish behaviour is closer to human behaviour, leaving the possibility that Cyphre is not so much a supernatural being as the evil inherent in humanity. By refusing to confirm Cyphre's supernatural status, the book actually implies the world has no order, there is no explanation, because that's just the way the world is. Parker's version implies that the society of the tail end of the eighties is more guilty of the crime of being able to alter one's identity for the sake of egocentrism and selfish material gain. By portraying Cyphre as the Devil it also implies that this is not the real state of humanity, it comes from somewhere else. The book on the other hand lays the blame at the door of the weak individual who has difficulty forming an identity and is unable to resist the pull of power and money, and unable to deal with all its ensuing trappings.

The book was written in 1978. The seventies was the era in which De

Niro came to prominence as a promising young actor. In Jack Kroll's seminal *Newsweek* article and interview with De Niro in 1977, a picture emerges of De Niro as an actor who is brilliantly adaptable to playing characters whose identities are in a state of flux or transformation. Kroll writes: "De Niro symbolizes the search for identity that has become pervasive and hectic in an uncertain America"[8]. De Niro's role in **Angel Heart** is interesting in its departure from his renowned roles in **Mean Streets, Godfather II, Taxi Driver, Raging Bull,** and so on. Louis Cyphre is an erudite articulate character who does not have to resort to inarticulate violence in order to get his point across. De Niro's portrayal of Cyphre is masterful in its subtle portrayal of changing mood, and underlying malicious intent. One reviewer commented, "De Niro demonically overacts in the part of Cyphre[9]". However, apart from the demonic costumery, De Niro actually underplays the role considering the possibilities. Roger Ebert has suggested that Cyphre looks "uncannily like Martin Scorsese... a wicked homage"[10].

De Niro's acting process is legendary, as is his dedication to his roles to the point of obsession (as noted by the director Elia Kazan), his "protean"[11] ability to play any role, and his incorporation of the Method, studied under Lee Strasberg and Stella Adler at The Actors Studio. Part of the power of De Niro's role in **Angel Heart** lies in the mystique that surrounds Robert De Niro; the air of danger, elusiveness, and his emotionally charged film roles where he plays volatile characters who can transform instantly (perhaps best demonstrated in **The Untouchables** in a sequence where, during dinner, he calmly pulls a baseball bat from under the table and smashes a colleague's head to a pulp). De Niro gives the film an extra quality of intensity. Jack Kroll notes that "De Niro always suggests positive energy that has been perverted"[12]. Lucifer has found his understudy in Robert De Niro, the "Special Guest" in **Angel Heart**.

NOTES

1. Sleeve notes, **Angel Heart** soundtrack, Island Visual Arts Ltd., 1987.

2. The music for **Angel Heart** was composed, arranged and conducted by Trevor Jones who also arranged the synthesizer music in the film. Courtney Pine provides instrumental music as well as featuring in "Rainy Days", Brownie McGhee's song which features in the film and was re-recorded for the film in New Orleans. Other songs include "Honeyman Blues" performed by Bessie Smith, "The Right Key, But The Wrong Keyhole" performed by Lilian Boutte, and "Soul On Fire" performed by LaVern Baker. Johnny Favorite's supposed 1930's hit "Girl Of My Dreams" recurs throughout the film, Parker wanted it to haunt the film in the same way that Harry is haunted by the song and Johnny himself; the song is performed by Glen Gray and the Casa Loma Orchestra, 1938. Gospel singing also features in the film. The film uses music as a narrative function to reinforce themes or pre-empt events, as well as creating atmospheric ambience.

3. For a fuller discussion of occult, Voodoo, and supernatural narrative symbols such as fans and lifts in **Angel Heart** see "The Devil You Know: Satanism in **Angel Heart**", by Carrol L. Fry in *Literature-Film Quarterly*, Vol.19, No.3, 1991.

4. Fry has noted that Angel's fear of chicken's functions as part of the film's symbolic play on Angel being subconsciously aware that he is Johnny Favorite; Favorite would have an aversion to eggs and chickens because as Cyphre has so charmingly illustrated by symbolic reference to his hard-boiled egg, eggs like souls can easily be wolfed down by the Devil. Chickens have a sacrificial function in both occult and Voodoo ceremonies, and Angel's appearance with his comical sunglasses and nose guard is not unlike a rather over-sized and clumsy chicken that has the effect of drawing attention to itself.

5. See Fry, C.L., "The Devil You Know: Satanism In **Angel Heart**", p.202.

6. Roger Ebert, "Angel Heart", *Chicago Sun-Times*, 3/6/1987.

7. Franco Moretti, *Signs Taken For Wonders*, Verso, London, 1997, 1st pub. 1983, p134.

8. Jack Kroll, "De Niro: A Star For The '70s", in *Newsweek*, May 16, 1977, p80.

9. Rita Kempsey, "Angel Heart", in the *Washington Post*, 6/3/1987.

10. Roger Ebert, "Angel Heart", *Chicago Sun-Times*, 3/6/1987.

11. Jack Kroll, "De Niro: A Star For The '70s", in *Newsweek*, May 16, 1977, p80.

12. Jack Kroll, "De Niro: A Star For The '70s", in *Newsweek*, May 16, 1977, p80.

CAPE FEAR REVISITED:
MITCHUM Vs DE NIRO

Cape Fear (1991), Martin Scorsese's seventh collaboration with Robert De Niro, is the story of a seemingly happy family terrorized by an ex-con, a menacing figure returning from an anguished past. It's also a remake of the 1962 thriller of the same name – adapted from the John D. Macdonald novel *The Executioners* – which starred Gregory Peck, Robert Mitchum, and Polly Bergen. The original version was intended as a Hitchcock project, but Hitchcock turned it down, and it was realized instead by Bristol-born filmmaker J. Lee Thompson, director of **Taras Bulba** and **The Guns Of Navarone**. Both versions tell the same story. A number of years after being imprisoned, vicious psychopath Max Cady emerges with a single-minded mission: to seek revenge on his attorney, Sam Bowden, by menacingly stalking Bowden's beautiful wife and teenage daughter.

Scorsese's first attempt at the thriller genre, **Cape Fear** – like most of the director's movies – typically focuses on the dangers and anxieties of his characters' private lives. As its title implies, **Cape Fear** is really a film about an emotional state – a state of fear, anxiety, and edginess. Although filmed in widescreen (the first of Scorsese's films to be shot this way), **Cape Fear** still maintains enough visceral strength and intimacy to accommodate a tremendous amount of tension. Much of it has the feel of a particularly intense personal nightmare.

The remake was a huge commercial hit, although critical reviews were mixed. Most critics agreed that the film was savagely suspenseful and scary, a thoughtfully crafted shocker. Many praised the nervous, agitated, expressionist quality of the camerawork, such as the obsessive use of close-ups and the dollying into empty spaces. Others praised the way in which Scorsese draws attention to the loneliness, guilt, and ultimate failure that all the characters in the film seem to face. Some found the world of the film highly believable; others described it as often implausible, yet suggested that much of our disbelief is distracted by the movie's performances and technical proficiency – the maelstrom of its rhythm and the film-conscious way it alludes to so much cinema history.

In *Variety*, Todd McCarthy noted that "[**Cape Fear**] clearly reps a case of Scorsese taking an obviously commercial project involving material outside his own interests", instead of being his own project, as his films typically are, and therefore – like most of his other films – crafted with a certain amount of artistic integrity. McCarthy adds that "**Cape Fear** is the most story-driven film he has ever made, as well as the one most rooted in genre". In *Newsweek*, David Ansen claimed that "[**Cape Fear**] gives you a pumped-up, thrill-happy ride (assuming you have a stomach for violent pulp), but it doesn't linger in the mind as Scorsese's richest movies do. It's a swell B-movie dressed in haute cinematic couture". And Ray Greene in *Village View* described **Cape Fear** as Scorsese's attempt to make an upscale "Nightmare On Elm Street" film, decked out in art-house mannerisms but introducing mainstream audiences to the sneering hero-villain, "past perpetrator of horrific crimes" à la Freddy Krueger[1].

In many ways, Scorsese's version of **Cape Fear** is not so much a remake as an homage to J. Lee Thompson's original movie. A number of actors from the original, for example, appear in cameo roles in the remake. Robert Mitchum, the original Max Cady, is recruited to play the chief of police, and Gregory Peck, the original straight-laced Sam Bowden, appears here as Cady's corrupt and disreputable criminal lawyer. Martin Balsam – Arbogast in **Psycho** and police chief Mark Dutton in the original **Cape Fear**, here turns up in a cameo role as a judge, and composer Elmer Bernstein adapts, orchestrates and re-cues Bernard Herrman's haunting, persistent score from the 1962 version. Significant elements of the original plot are also maintained by Scorsese. In both versions, the characters deal with similar moral dilemmas, and face similar tests of strength and vision. It also becomes gradually clear in both movies that what Cady intends to do is to drive Bowden's family apart, by cleverly exploiting their pre-existing conflicts and internal rivalries.

There are also, however, a number of significant differences between Thompson's original and Scorsese's remake, and while most of these differences are to do with performance, others are issues of plot, theme and motif. The 1962 version, for example, plays around with a nautical theme, and not just during the deadly showdown on the houseboat at **Cape Fear**. Robert Mitchum's Max Cady takes a cheap room at the docks, hangs out with sailors at the dock taverns, and gets beaten up by Bowden's hired thugs under the pier. The most menacing scenes in this movie are made additionally threatening through the use of loud noises – the angry churning of motorboat engines on the marina, and the thunderous rolling noises of the bowling alley. And Bowden's daughter Nancy seems much younger than fifteen, which makes Cady's lascivious oglings all the more unpalatable ("she's getting to be almost as juicy as your wife", he comments to Bowden, maliciously).

The 1962 version also brings up some interesting legal issues centring around the inadequacies of the law. For want of any other charge, for example, Dutton plans to arrest Cady on charges of "lewd vagrancy" when private dick Charlie Sievers (Telly Savalas) observes him picking up a girl in a bar and taking her back to a hotel. This scene is particularly interesting

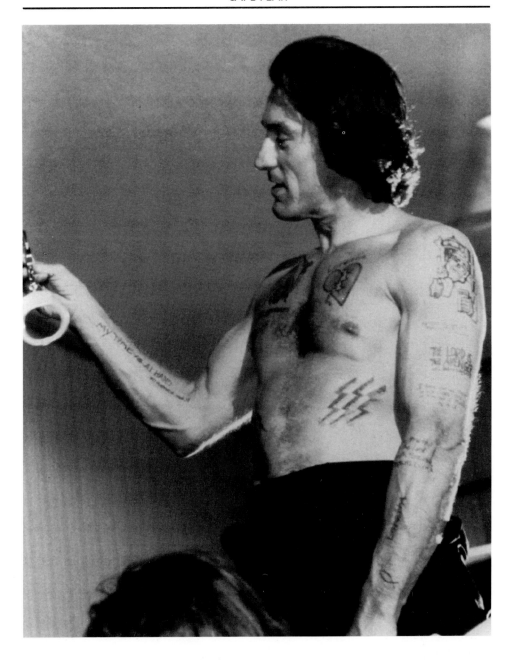

because of what it suggests, rather than what it shows. We never see what Cady does to the bar girl, and she refuses ever to speak of it. Instead, beaten and bruised, she packs her bags and heads out of town immediately ("do you think that I could ever, ever, to another human soul, step up and tell what that man did?" she asks Savalas. "Something horrible..."). This hinting at implicitly unspeakable barbarities seems to suggest that Mitchum's Cady is the owner of truly evil, perhaps even Mephistophelean powers.

Scorsese's version, however, introduces additional features of psychological complexity into the film's plot. We learn, for example, that Scorsese's Bowden (Nick Nolte) was once Cady's defense attorney, and that he purposefully withheld evidence that might have let his dangerous client go free. Cady cannot forgive him for this lapse of justice, and Bowden, himself less than honest, is thereby largely responsible for bringing Cady's wrath down upon himself and his family. In Scorsese's film, moreover, the bar girl Cady rapes and beats becomes Bowden's cast-off mistress (Illeana Douglas), a court clerk who goes to bed with Cady only because Bowden has left her alone and lonely. Again, Bowden is made partly responsible for her plight, suggesting that the lawyer is far from an innocent victim of Cady's motiveless malignancy.

Consequently, Thompson's tale of vigilante justice is elaborated by Scorsese into a tightly-crafted psychological web, ironic and full of dread. Gregory Peck's straight-arrow southern gentleman becomes Nick Nolte's affluent neurotic – a man who, having committed an ethical transgression in the belief that it was the right thing to do, is now haunted by his tormented past. As a result, he's forced to question his own belief in the strength and power of the law, and ultimately finds himself responding to Cady on Cady's own terms. Recognizing his own weaknesses, Bowden is ultimately horrified to face the savagery to which his own hypocrisy has forced him to descend.

Scorsese also presents Bowden as the center of an already dysfunctional family, weakened by pre-existing tensions, merely waiting for an outside force to arrive and disrupt an already unbalanced situation. His wife Leigh (Jessica Lange) is uptight and resentful, and the pair have raging fights in their bedroom, witnessed by their troubled adolescent daughter Danielle (Juliette Lewis). In constant conflict with both her parents, Danielle has recently been suspended from school for smoking pot. This presentation of a family trapped in the confines of an environment that defines and often stifles them, allows Scorsese to ask some pertinent questions about the nature of role-playing and identity – about the acting that takes place in the reality of families and communities, as well as in film and in theatre.

The most significant difference between the original **Cape Fear** and its 1991 remake, however, lies in the respective performances of Robert Mitchum and Robert De Niro in the role of the psychopathic stalker, Max Cady.

Mitchum's Max Cady is a big, handsome, imposing fellow in a white suit and white Panama hat. Eight years in jail have left him with an impressive knowledge of the law; he knows his rights, and consequently exudes a menacing self-confidence. He's a smooth talker, but his eloquence betrays the constant threat of potential violence. "I like to put values on things, like the value of eight years, and the value of a family", he sneers at Bowden when they meet in a dockside tavern. "Interesting calculations, eh counsellor?"

Bowden calls him a "shocking degenerate" who "makes me sick to breathe the same air", which makes Cady laugh – a loud, chilling, bruised, twisted laugh. And yet despite his sociopathic violence, there is something almost charming about Mitchum's Cady – his dimpled chin, his twinkling eyes, the cheeky way he chews the butt of his huge cigars. Something in his jaunty walk and cool demeanour give to Mitchum's Max Cady a sensuality that De Niro never quite manages to pull off.

Nor, perhaps, does his intend to, for De Niro's Max Cady is an altogether different kind of animal, less laconic southern villain than white-trash terrorist, his body pumped up with muscle and festooned with a travesty of garishly coloured tattoos. De Niro lifted weights to add muscle to his body for the part of Cady, claiming "I feel if you're going to do certain parts, you really have to commit to them all the way to make them special"[2]. *Variety's* Todd McCarthy was impressed. "Cackling crazy at times, quietly purposeful and logical at others," writes McCarthy, "Cady is a sickie, utterly determined in his righteous cause, and De Niro plays him with tremendous relish, and is extremely funny in several scenes". And according to J. Hoberman in *The Village Voice*:

"De Niro's Cady is less the snake in the Bowden family Eden, more the projection of their unconscious fears. A cross splayed across his back, a Stalin pin-up on his cell wall, he's a self-taught nut-job, as much a mythological beast as a unicorn or yeti. Cady's release from prison is heralded by a drumroll of thunder. He's the return of Bowden's repressed... Cady is two-bit de Sade with delusions of grandeur. He sees himself as avenging angel ...Hair slicked back under a white yachting cap, mouth wrapped around the world's biggest stogie, tattooed torso draped in a flannel aloha shirt, half-camping on his Southern drawl, De Niro is a cracker from hell... The conception is wildly baroque – and most of the time, De Niro's more crazy than menacing... His Max Cady is a riff, and he never lets you forget it."

And in *Newsweek*, David Ansen claims that "it is De Niro – his body covered with tattoos and the tackiest wardrobe in the New South – who dominates the film with his lip-smacking, blackly comic, and terrifying portrayal of psychopathic self-righteousness"[3]. De Niro himself noted that his depiction of Cady – for which he received a Best Actor Academy Award nomination – is a portrayal of a man who is "incessant". "He just keeps coming and coming," observes De Niro. "What's terrifying is the idea that you can't stop

someone no matter what you do. He's like the Alien or the Terminator"[4]. Cady is indeed imbued with a remorseless inhuman quality, and in this respect may perhaps be seen as a precursive template of De Niro's later portrayal of the Frankenstein monster.

Interestingly, De Niro appropriates certain aspects of Mitchum's earlier performance as Cady – the mad laughter, the big cigars, the jaunty outfits, the cod accent – and exaggerates them almost to the point of the grotesque. But De Niro's Max Cady is more cocky and cool than Mitchum's, more smart and sarcastic, sneery in a slick, menacing way, more mannered, more muscular. He's also more audacious, composing his face into a charming, quizzical expression as he swings upside down on the parallel bars, talking to Danielle on the phone. At times he can be equally charming and likeable as Mitchum's Cady, even sweet, where Mitchum is grossly sensual.

A new aspect of Cady that De Niro introduces to the role is his unswerving evangelism. De Niro's Max Cady is a crazed Pentecostal revivalist – who speaks in tongues even as he drowns – akin to, and possibly even partly modelled on, Mitchum's itinerant killer-preacher in **The Night Of The Hunter** (1955). Obsessed with revenge, De Niro's Cady has spent four years in prison studying law and reading the Bible, turning himself into a hideous instrument of retribution. The elaborate tattoos that cover his body are almost all religious in nature, including the scales of Truth and Justice, and the Biblical phrases "Justice is Mine", "The Time is at Hand", and "Time the Avenger". Screenwriter Wesley Strick says that in the revised version of Max Cady, he wanted to create a psychopath "who has a real sense about himself being on a religious quest. The vengeance that he's seeking is pure and just and cleansing. Not only for him, but for Sam too. He absolutely believes that he's Sam's doom, but he's also Sam's redemption"[5]. Cady seems himself as a vehicle of divine retribution, and unlike many of the other characters in the film, does not pretend to be apart from or unaffected by the violence and degradation that surrounds him. Still, some reviewers remained unimpressed. In the *New Yorker*, Terence Rafferty complained that "De Niro's frenetic but thoroughly uninteresting performance is emblematic of the movie's inadequacy. He's covered with tattooed messages and symbols, but he doesn't seem to have a body. We could feel Mitchum's evil in all its slimy physicality. De Niro's is an evil that we merely read".

Other performances, as well as De Niro's, also contribute to the convincing power of the remake. Jessica Lange makes Polly Bergen's glamorous suburban wife into an angry, sardonic character with a streak of discontentment which fuels both her mistrust of her husband, and her reluctant fascination with Cady's motives. She bickers constantly with her husband and daughter, cigarette in hand, and snorts smoke through her nose angrily.

Gregory Peck plays Sam Bowden as a straight-laced, uptight family man, obsessed with his property and his possessions (which, he seems to believe, include his wife and daughter). He wags his finger at Cady like an angry father ("now you listen to me..."), and strides around his house in a white towelling dressing gown over his business suit. In contrast, Nolte's

Bowden in unsteady in the face of danger. As Cady's assault on his family grows more vicious and more intense, Nolte becomes frantic and twitchy, pacing around desperately, sweating, chain-smoking, pushing his glasses up the bridge of his nose repetitively in a gesture of nervous anticipation.

After De Niro's, however, the performance that most critics draw attention to is that of Juliette Lewis as the Bowdens' teenage daughter Danielle. Perhaps this is because his scenes with Lewis allow De Niro's Cady to mellow into a crafty demonic villain, instead of the white-trash Bible-spouting psychopath he incarnates in most of the film. Lewis's Danielle is far more rebellious and sexually aware than Lori Martin's Nancy in the 1962 version. Nancy is a vulnerable little daddy's girl; Danni is a foxy temptress in a tight dress, chewing her finger coquettishly, lying around in her underwear, swinging her body from side to side, her face twisted into a libidinous smirk. Her response to Cady's attempted seductions (first on the phone, then in person, in the guise of her new drama teacher) is one of giggly, half-terrified flirtatiousness, which makes Cady appear even more chilling and distasteful than usual.

The remake is also faithful to the original in that the ending to both movies is really something of an anti-climax. The "deadly showdown at Cape Fear" in the 1962 version is updated into a lengthy and melodramatic final confrontation between Cady and the Bowden family at night, on the water, in the middle of a torrential storm. This sequence, which lasts approximately fifteen minutes on the screen, apparently took two weeks to film, and necessitated the construction of a ninety-foot long water tank (to avoid the potential problems caused by the weather and tides, not to mention alligators[6]). In terms of filming, this final scene is the most logistically complex of the entire picture, involving a difficult series of rapidly-paced cuts and very dramatic camera moves, including turns, tracking shots, and so on.

Yet in both versions of **Cape Fear**, this dramatic final scene is less interesting than many of the other, quieter sequences which allow the tension to develop through the performances of the individual actors, rather than through cinematic pyrotechnics. Scenes like the one in which Robert Mitchum strips sleazily down to his shorts in the police station, or the one in which De Niro seductively entices Juliette Lewis on to the school stage with his intoxicating cigar smoke, are more dramatic, emotionally, than any number of disorienting camera angles. Perhaps where the original version tends to underplay certain scenes and episodes, the remake tends to overplay them somewhat. However, if **Cape Fear** is an emotional state, it is a remarkable tribute to both Mitchum and De Niro that they both manage to evoke that same ·state, and those same emotions, through two greatly contrasting, intensely distinctive performances.

NOTES

1. All reviews cit in Douglas Brode, **The Films Of Robert De Niro**, Citadel Press, NY 1993, 231–234.

2. Cit in Brode, 234.

3. All reviews cit in ibid., 232.

4. Cit in ibid., 234.

5. Wesley Strick, cit in David Morgan, "Return To Cape Fear", *Los Angeles Times Calendar*, February 1991.

6. Ibid.

MANN'S WORLD:
HOW DE NIRO AND PACINO
GENERATED 'HEAT'

Two middle-aged men – a cop and a criminal – engage in a battle of wills on the streets of contemporary Los Angeles, supported by a squad of detectives and a gang of crooks respectively. Each has a grudging respect for the other's talent and dedication, but the town ain't big enough for both of them. After police surveillance fails to trap the gang, a tip from an informant reveals the location of their next blag. A gunfight ensues, with fatalities on both sides. Just as it seems the leader of the gang will make his getaway, the desire for vengeance against the informer proves too strong. Despite eliminating his foe, the criminal is himself subsequently shot and killed by the cop. Described in those terms, this seems a pretty unremarkable synopsis, but from such over familiar material was fashioned the best crime movie of the decade.

CRIMINAL GENIUS

At a time in cinema history when postmodernism and irony exerted their influence to an almost tyrannical degree, writer/director Michael Mann did a brave and remarkable thing. He made a modernist picture. **Heat** was a sprawling epic of crime and punishment which looked to Dickens, and Dostoevsky, Jung and Sartre for inspiration, rather than the lurid Black Mask magazine detective stories which served as template for **Pulp Fiction**. Dazzling Tarantino's L.A. underworld portmanteau may have been, but Hollywood needed somebody to make an unashamedly serious, even sombre movie. (**Heat** was vital in this respect, if only to serve as a stark alternative to the ludicrous likes of Oliver Stone's **Natural Born Killers** – the cinematic equivalent of watching a middle-aged aunt dancing to techno at a family wedding.) Mann invested his characters with a code of honour, a defiantly masculine pride, and an explicitly declared existential philosophy with which to justify their actions.

To play these men of stature and integrity, the director needed actors who took themselves and their craft seriously, and who carried weight with the audience. A former disco dancer on the comeback trail and an action star looking for indie cred simply would not do. For **Heat** to work, we needed to believe that a man could achieve greatness as cop or criminal, and that meant casting the only two individuals of their generation who had achieved undeniable greatness as actors.

Al Pacino signed up to play Vincent Hanna of the L.A.P.D, and Robert

De Niro took on the role of his criminal nemesis, Neil McCauley.

OPENING SHOTS

Much is made of the similarities between the two protagonists, but initially it's the differences between the men which are most apparent. As the opening credits roll over Dante Spinotti's luminous images of the city at night, we see McCauley moving purposefully through the urban landscape. Although constantly looking left and right, he is careful not to make eye contact with his fellow Angelenos, and since we never see the city from Neil's point of view, we can assume that he is not observing and reacting to his environment in any significant fashion. Unlike, say Travis Bickle, Neil is a loner by choice, a self-sufficient, self-contained individual who is not looking to forge any connection with the world around him. De Niro's features betray no feeling other than grim determination, his mouth is set in a line, behind a neatly trimmed beard. His mission – the theft of an ambulance to be used in a heist – is accomplished with the minimum of fuss, and immediately it is clear that this is a can-do guy, an isolated model of efficiency.

Contrast this with Pacino's first appearance. Vincent Hanna is first presented *in flagrante*, making love to his beautiful, neurotic wife. The morning light reflects from the jewelry adorning his neck and wrists, and his wife's hands clutch passionately at his impressively and, one suspects, expensively styled hairdo. When leaving for work with indecent haste, his gun and badge are proudly displayed. This is a peacock of a man, and if Neil is powered by strength of will, then Vincent is driven by the force of his personality. Pacino was criticised at the time of the film's release for being wild of eye and flared of nostril, but his performance is every bit as suited to the role as De Niro's measured stillness.

In the armoured car robbery sequence which sets up the conflict between the two central characters, Mann takes an enormous risk, and gets away with it. McCauley earns our respect for his slick coordination of the hold-up, at least up to the point where new recruit Waingro loses his cool and shoots an unarmed guard. Chris (Val Kilmer) turns to his leader, who authorises the execution of the other witnesses with a nod of the head. It's a moment of brutality, and one which could have cost McCauley the audience's sympathy and robbed the resulting running time (nearly three hours) of the moral complexity required to elevate it above the good guys against bad guys formula common to the genre. In a stroke of genius, the director has McCauley absolved of any charges of psychopathological trigger happiness by the very person who would be expected to feel outrage on behalf of society – the cop. The moment Hanna arrives on the scene he starts expressing admiration for the larcenous crew, differentiating between their

standing in the criminal fraternity and that of mere "gangbangers". "Robbery Homicide is taking this case," he says, relishing the chance to confront a worthy opponent. He then goes on to describe accurately the heist we have just witnessed – including the execution – with undisguised respect for the professionalism and daring on display.

The moral universe of the film is thus established: murder is a regrettable but sometimes inevitable consequence of the high stakes game McCauley and his cohorts play. If the guardians of law and order find his behaviour acceptable, who are we to argue. A degree of ethical subtlety is added to the mix with the gang's decision to kill the psychopath, Waingro, partly because his loose cannon nature represents a security risk, but also because he has broken their own code by indulging in indiscriminate slaughter. Significant too that it is McCauley himself who plans to carry out the death sentence, rather than entrusting it to one of his lieutenants. This further establishes his credentials as a leader of men and setter of standards, but the cold fury in his eyes hints that perhaps he is capable of emotion after all. Allowing Waingro to escape is the first mistake McCauley makes, and in the life or death (under)world of the criminal community, it proves fatal for the entire gang.

KINGS OF THE URBAN JUNGLE

The director's daring extends further than the seriousness of his tone or the scope of his story. Where so many of his contemporaries slavishly follow mythic archetypes, Mann has the confidence to adapt myth to fit his characters and narrative rather than vice versa. From its origins in prehistory, through classical drama, medieval romance, Elizabethan theatre, hefty realist novels from the turn of the last century to the postmodern age of irony at the end of this, story-telling has followed a particular model. A young hero (or anti-hero in certain texts) learns from a mentor, proves his worth in combat, and violently usurps an aging power-monger father figure to claim his rightful place as lord protector of all he surveys. It's a blueprint adhered to in everything from **Apocalypse Now** to the **Star Wars** trilogy, but **Heat** chooses a different path.

McCauley and Hanna are not idealistic youths out to prove their macho worth. Instead they are warrior generals, possessing the wisdom of age yet still clearly virile. (Imagine Colonel Kilgore going up river to face Colonel Kurtz, or Obi Wan Kenobi duking it out with Emperor Palpatine.) They are father figures to their respective "crews", but their position as leaders is never questioned, let alone threatened. Hanna doesn't have the stereotypical gruff superior officer to answer to, and McCauley's relationship with Nate – despite their age difference – is one of equals, rather than master and pupil. Pacino it is who gets to save the damsel in distress, but in this case she is his own step-daughter, rather than a prospective mate. The biggest departure from the mythic archetype however, comes in the relationship between Chris and Neil. Far from desiring independence, Val Kilmer's character is desperate to remain subservient to the older man. After arguing with his hot-headed, adulterous wife, Chris seeks solace and sanctuary in Neil's austere, unfurnished beach house like a child returning to the family home. When Neil later announces that the bank hold-up will be his last score, the camera cuts to a hurt and bewildered Chris, his face like that of a son about to be abandoned by his father. This is clearly not a young prince destined for power, and it comes as no surprise when, instead of assuming Neil's mantle, he ends the film in exile, a cripple and a cuckold.

In a film unashamedly obsessed with exploring the nature of masculinity, it is McCauley who is presented as the ideal embodiment of male values. This would not have been the case had he remained the isolated individual we see in the early scenes, but as the film progresses so too do Neil's relationships and capacity for emotional involvement. In the aforementioned scene with Chris at the beach house, he wonders aloud why the younger man doesn't leave his wife, since all the couple seem to do is tear into each other. The reply – "For me the sun rises and sets with her, man" – seems to mean nothing to Neil who responds with his own credo: "Do not have any attachments, do not have anything in your life you are not willing to walk out on in 30 seconds flat if you spot the heat around the corner." In many ways this is the key line in the film, in that it's Neil's gradual abandonment of this belief system which accounts for his character development. There's no doubt that Neil has paternal feelings for Chris. Confronting Charlene at the scene of her infidelity, he orders her to give the marriage another chance. This may at first glance appear to be another example of the leader's "nobody rocks the boat" control-freak tendencies, and he certainly leaves Charlene no choice in the matter. However he also guarantees that if things don't work out, he will underwrite a future for Chris's wife and child. There's no reason why Neil's scheme couldn't come into play immediately, but he clearly recognises the importance of the relationship to Chris, and wants to save him any distress. Far from removing "attachments" from the younger man's life, he is ensuring that Chris has something he will never be "willing to walk out on". The irony is that Charlene only gets to prove her love for Chris by helping facilitate his escape, at great risk to her own liberty. We know that both will be devastated by separation, so it's definitely not a case of Chris adopting Neil's motto. By that stage of the film, of course, Neil himself has ceased to believe in the worth of a solitary existence, thanks to Eady.

LOVE AND BULLETS

The love affair between the master criminal and the graphic design graduate is beautifully constructed and performed. Their first meeting sets the tone, with Neil initially suspicious and then embarrassed when he realises that this is not an undercover cop but a vulnerable young woman with a romantic interest in him. De Niro's performance in this scene amounts to a master class in non-verbal acting: it's as though his thoughts and conflicting emotions are written in bold type across his face. When he does speak, the words come in halting fashion, and his shortcomings in the art of small talk are cruelly exposed. Eady too is awkward and tentative, but even she is able to fluster Neil with an emotionally direct exchange:

Eady: You travel a lot?
Neil: Yeah.
Eady: Does it make you lonely?
Neil: I am alone, I'm not lonely.

This of course, marks the beginning of Neil's realisation that he actually *is* lonely. Their subsequent love scene reveals yet more about each character's

needs. As Neil pulls her to him, Eady may feel that he is being masterful and protective of her, but his embrace seems to envelop her, as though he were desperate to absorb her into his self and fill the chasm therein. Afterwards, once we've glimpsed De Niro's impressively muscular torso (again, no need for a younger man to fight this king's battles) he slopes away, leaving Eady sleeping.

Although he tries to remove all traces of his presence in her life – he wraps a glass in a handkerchief to avoid fingerprints – it's soon apparent that forgetting this woman will not be easy. He calls her and they date again. He is confident enough to tell Hanna of her existence with some pride, and most significantly of all, financing a new life with Eady becomes the reason he carries out the absurdly risky final heist. Instead of a lover being something to walk away *from*, she becomes someone to run away *with*.

One thing doesn't change for Neil: his need for absolute loyalty. When Eady learns of his lawless lifestyle, her lover offers a stark choice. She can leave him now, or stay with him forever. There would be no chance of an amicable break-up once they had established their new identities, and any separation then would be of a permanent nature. At least she can't accuse the guy of fearing commitment.

COFFEE, ANYONE?

Despite the heists, gun battles, revenge killings, and love scenes which occur throughout the film, for most people the most thrilling ten minutes in **Heat** take place over a civilised cup of coffee. This is the moment the protagonists finally meet, but more than that it marks the first time in their careers Robert De Niro and Al Pacino act opposite each other. From the second the project was announced in the trades, this was the scene film enthusiasts were desperate to see. Both are terrific in the scene, and it's no criticism of their performances to suggest a blurring of the distinction between actor and character, as De Niro/McCauley and Pacino/Hanna indulge in some mutual admiration. There is a playful side to the dialogue, even when they are threatening to kill each other should the situation arise:

Hanna: You know, we are sitting here face to face like a couple of regular fellows and if I have to go out there and put you down, I'll tell you, I won't like it. But if it's between you and some poor bastard whose wife you're gonna turn into a widow, brother, you are going down.
McCauley: There is a flip side to that coin. What if you do get me boxed in and I will have to put you down? Cause no matter what, you will not get in my way. We've been face to face, yeah. But I will not hesitate, not for a second.

It's during this good-natured but deadly serious banter that we see De Niro's trademark eye-wrinkling smile, as he enjoys the scene almost despite himself.

If the coffee shop conversation is fascinating for cineastes and students of screen acting, it's of equal interest to philosophy scholars. The scene would've been indulgent and worthless had the two stars simply bumped egos and traded quips, but it is in fact essential to the film as a whole. It is here that the characters explicitly outline the existential motivation behind every action they take.

Neil: I do what I do best, I take scores. You do what you do best, try to stop guys like me.

Hanna nods in agreement, and the bond between the two is established. Each realises that he is defined by his own actions, yet at the same time requires the other to give these actions meaning. What's more, each consciously relishes their role in the drama, as proved in the following, somewhat perverse exchange. Remember, this is a police lieutenant talking to a criminal whom he strongly suspects of at least three murders:

McCauley:	Maybe we should both be doing something else, pal.
Hanna:	I don't know how to do anything else.
McCauley:	Neither do I.
Hanna:	I don't much want too either.
McCauley:	Neither do I.

There is even contempt for the Johnny Six Pack, Sally Housecoat ordinary decent god-fearing law abiding citizens who pay their wages and line their pockets. Both reject out of hand the cosy domesticity of a "normal type life". With typically shrewd directorial judgement, Mann doesn't show the men finish up their beverage and head for the exit. Seeing them jump in their respective cars and say *adios* would've been something of an anti-climax and robbed their final confrontation of the necessary impact. We know that when next these individuals – who could easily have been friends under different circumstances – meet, one or both is going to die bloodily.

TWILIGHT OF THE GODS

And so it comes to pass – but not before De Niro has one final moment of solitary glory. Driving to freedom, his girl at his side, McCauley receives word that Waingro, the rat responsible for the deaths of his friends, is in hiding at a hotel near the airport. He doesn't change course at first, but we gradually see his features contort in silent rage, and he veers abruptly across the freeway and into a long, luminous tunnel. It lights the way to his own death.

Waingro is located and dispensed with, executioner style, but Neil pays a high price for his vengeance. The police have the psychopath under surveillance, and soon McCauley is being pursued on foot by Hanna. In a final reversal of his previous beliefs, Neil leaves Eady not because he doesn't care about her, but because he knows the end is near and he doesn't want her implicated in his crimes or witness to his demise.

The chase culminates in a field near an airport runway. As jets land and take off, the night sky becomes flooded with light, and it is during just such an instance of illumination that Vincent shoots Neil. The criminal is dying, but the cop takes no pleasure in victory. McCauley's last words may be defiant (he says he swore he'd never go back to the penitentiary) but his final gesture is conciliatory. He holds out his hand and the cop takes it, glad that his worthy adversary does not have to die alone. On the soundtrack, Moby's music reaches a crescendo, Neil breathes his last and... That's it. Credits roll. We never discover the fate of Chris and Charlene, or Eady, or whether Vincent makes a better fist of his marriage. Again, this is a masterstroke on Mann's part, for by ending the film with the death of one protagonist, he shows that the world which existed within the film is no

more. This was a world only made possible by the twin forces of Vincent and Neil, and when one man died, it was the end of the world for both of them.

ODD MAN OUT:
ROBERT DE NIRO/LOUIS GARA IN 'JACKIE BROWN'

Quentin Tarantino's third feature film as director is a departure from both **Reservoir Dogs** and **Pulp Fiction**; where his debut and follow up were dynamic, highly stylised and self-consciously cinematic ("movie movies", as he calls them), **Jackie Brown** is lower key but is also a more assured film. All three films boast top-grade ensemble casts giving appropriately fine performances, but where script, cinematography, soundtrack and editorial flair impress in **Reservoir Dogs** and **Pulp Fiction**, the emphasis in **Jackie Brown** is on character and performance. Almost single-handedly bridging the gap between arthouse and multiplex cinema audiences, Tarantino himself became the star of his first two films. The characters of these films perform for their director within the confines of their plots, respectively a failed bank robbery and a series of interlocking crime tales. By contrast, the first 90 minutes of **Jackie Brown** are devoted to character development, out of which the plot grows. The remaining running time focuses on "the action", a money exchange which is viewed through the multiple perspectives of various characters. In **Jackie Brown**, Tarantino takes a back seat to his cast.

Adapted by Tarantino from the Elmore Leonard novel *Rum Punch*, the director has stated his wish to retain the essence of the book. While there are some major alterations – most notably the eponymous heroine, written into the script with Grier in mind – the screenplay is faithful to the novel in terms of its emphasis on character. Specifically, Tarantino has taken a leaf from Leonard's book with his use of naturalistic dialogue. "Characters talking around things as opposed to talking about them... the way real people talk", explains Tarantino. Of course, Tarantino's own characters are known for their verbal gymnastics, think of Steve Buscemi's motormouth Mr. Pink or Samuel L. Jackson's gospel-spewing Jules. Nevertheless, and although Ordell the entrepreneurial gun dealer (Jackson once again) is an exception, in **Jackie Brown** there is an easing off on this kind of verbosity. Where the dialogue of the earlier films is spat out like bullets from a gun, in **Jackie Brown** it's poured out like a cup of java. Furthermore, **Jackie Brown**'s characters talk less about everything from comic books to television cop shows (i.e. kitsch pop culture) and more about the everyday mundanities of life: vinyl versus CD, hair grafts, retirement – it's a move from the dynamic to the domestic.

Viewed in this context, Robert De Niro's character, Louis Gara is the odd one out in **Jackie Brown**. Louis is defined, not through dialogue, but rather the lack of it, not through action, rather inactivity, not even through

the camera's gaze, instead Louis is backgrounded or sidelined in the *mise en scène*. Where all of the featured characters, major and minor, are aggressively proactive, Louis is, apart from the shooting of Melanie, passive and reactive – and barely that. According to Tarantino, Jackie is the focus of the film – all the action centres on her. Max represents the audience point of view, while Ordell is the rhythm of the film. Louis represents none of these things; he's backgrounded and in the dark about the proceedings much of the time. What happens, happens in spite of Louis. In fact, Louis might be seen as the negative of his boss and friend, Ordell; Ordell being animated, verbose, commanding, Louis being comatose, reticent, subservient. (Interestingly, Tarantino has made Ordell a lot smarter than he is in *Rum Punch* and the other Leonard novel he appears in, *The Switch*. Louis, on the other hand, is dumbed down and certainly appears far less clued-up than he does in *Rum Punch*.) This positioning of Louis emphasises his background: a habitual criminal who has spent most of his life in and out of various correctional institutions. By what is now his middle age, Louis is a fish out of water outside of the prison regime.

In **Jackie Brown**'s opening scene – not the credit sequence with

Jackie entering the airport, but Ordell, Louis and Melanie at Ordell's beach house – Ordell raps on at length about his business while Louis listens. The scene lasts for seven minutes during which time Louis mutters a total of 13 monosyllabic responses to Ordell, the longest of which, clocking in two minutes into the scene, is "Who's your partner?". In the next scene Ordell and Louis visit Max Cherry at his bail bonds office. While Ordell discusses business with Max, Louis loafs around in the background, flips through a magazine, helps himself to some coffee and eventually goes to wait in Ordell's car. There are two significant points to be made here: One, Louis appears in the first two scenes of the film. Two, he apparently contributes, in either word or action, very little.

Jackie Brown is a film about multiple points of view. Louis' view of the events and relationships between the other characters is partial at best, but remains ignorant for the most part. How the various characters act depends on their view of what's going on around them. This is made most apparent during the money exchange, viewed, first from Jackie's point of view, then Louis and Melanie's and finally Max's. Jackie and her accomplice Max are "in the know", having masterminded the operation. Melanie is clear about what she wants from the exchange (i.e. to double-cross Ordell), but the whole thing perplexes Louis. This partial view is the key to understanding Louis' character; it's indicative of it and a prime motivating force for both his actions and his inactivity. For this reason, it's worth taking some time to see things from Louis' partial point of view. To that end I want to provide an alternative synopsis of the film, one that doesn't start from an objective point of view, but from a subjective one, from Louis'.

Just out of prison, where he served time for a bank robbery, Louis hooks up with old friend Ordell Robbie, whom he has previously done time with. Ordell invites Louis to stay at his beach house where he meets one of Ordell's girls, Melanie, whom he last saw when she was 14 years old. Melanie is impressed by his involvement in a bank robbery. Ordell boasts about his gun running business. Later, Louis accompanies Ordell to bail bondsman Max Cherry's office, but ends up waiting in the car while Ordell and Max do business. Later still, Ordell sets up Louis with another of his girls, Simone, who entertains him with a Diana Ross impersonation at her apartment. Ordell interrupts with a phone call and asks Louis to join him, rather confusingly, in the street outside. Ordell opens the boot of his car to reveal the body of an ex-employee named Beaumont he has murdered, after which he asks Louis to come in on his business, which he agrees to. The next day, Ordell buys Louis some new clothes and he relaxes back at the beach house, smoking grass with Melanie and having sex with her after Ordell has left. After getting re-acquainted, Melanie proposes they rip off Ordell. Later, in a bar, Louis warns Ordell about Melanie's disloyalty and confesses to having sex with her,

neither of which seems to bother Ordell. Louis meets Jackie Brown when she visits Ordell at the beach house; her and Ordell argue outside while he watches television, make up, then fill Louis in on the money exchange plan. Meanwhile, Melanie's ongoing badgering starts to irritate him and later becomes infuriating when she delays them leaving for the money exchange, for which Ordell badmouths him over the phone. Things get worse in Melanie's van on the way to the shopping mall and they arrive late, by which time Louis is sweating with nerves. Melanie makes the switch with Jackie in the changing room of a woman's boutique, during which time Louis notices the bail bondsman, Cherry. Melanie leaves in a rush, but Louis catches up and takes the bag with the money in it. In the car park, Louis forgets where the van is parked and when Melanie winds him up about it, he shoots her. Later, Louis picks Ordell up in the van and admits to killing Melanie. Ordell isn't too bothered, but is furious to discover most of the money missing. He accuses Louis of double-crossing him, which Louis denies. They work out that Jackie probably has the money and then Ordell shoots Louis.

Louis barely has time to work out both himself and Ordell have been double-crossed by Jackie before he is killed. Thus, Louis' partial view is his undoing. Key to Ordell's murderous anger and disappointment in Louis is the fact that Louis saw Max during the money exchange, but failed to put two and two together at the time. "Why should I think something's weird if I don't know nothing about it?" asks Louis. Indeed, Louis didn't know that Jackie and Max knew each other, although he momentarily questioned Max's presence at the site of the money exchange. Of course, if Louis hadn't gone and sat in the car during scene two at Max's office, he might have overheard Ordell and the bail bondsman talking about Jackie. Instead, Louis remains ignorant and takes no action during the money exchange.

In an interview published in *Sight And Sound* magazine Tarantino noted that, "you know every script will have four to six basic scenes that you're going to do. But it's the scenes in the middle that you've got to write through – that's where your characters really come from." Apart from the opening scene, the scene in which Louis kills Melanie and the one in which he himself is killed by Ordell, all of Louis' scenes are what Tarantino describes as "scenes in the middle". In keeping with Tarantino's take on character development, Louis becomes a fully defined character as much through the "middle" scenes as through the "basic" ones he appears in. The scenes that feature Louis hanging out at Ordell's beach house, where little "happens" apart from watching television and smoking grass with Melanie, become as important as his death scene and the murder of Melanie. Thus, Louis' screen presence is at once insignificant and significant; he's a minor player in terms of exposition, but a major one in terms of characterisation. And so, during the course of the opening scene referred to earlier, we learn much about Louis' character: he's an ex-con; a habitual criminal and a two-time looser; he's out of touch with life outside prison; he's unambitious, shifty and somewhat uptight; and he's sex-starved (check his furtive glances at Melanie's feet). We learn all this in just two short scenes, totalling around 10 minutes running time. For all intents and purposes, Louis is a B-movie character being played by an A-list actor.

Tarantino has made a habit of casting his screen idols in his films: Harvey Keitel in **Reservoir Dogs**, John Travolta in **Pulp Fiction**, Pam Grier in **Jackie Brown** – in each case reviving the career of the star in question. With De Niro it's a different story. Although he's had his share of critical and box office flops, just a few years before working with Tarantino, De Niro had appeared in such high profile films as **Heat** and **Casino**. Where the screen personas of the other actors mentioned were reinvented or revitalised with charismatic roles, in **Jackie Brown** the opposite is true of De Niro; his own considerable persona is played down. In contrast to the charismatic parts De Niro has played in the past – the psychotic Travis Bickle in **Taxi Driver**, bestial Jake La Motta in **Raging Bull**, smooth operator Ace Rothstein in **Casino** – Louis Gara is introverted, and De Niro gives an appropriately introspective performance.

Although Louis convinces as a fully rounded character, we are not, for the most part, privy to his thoughts or feelings. We read De Niro's performance, understand the character, in terms of motivation, history, etc., but we are rarely certain what's going on at any specific time inside Louis' head. As expressive as De Niro's performance is, it is also a remarkably controlled one in which the actor ensures that Louis remains opaque. This is why Louis' sudden shooting of Melanie towards the end of the film comes as a surprise. There are warning signs: Louis' nervousness prior to the money exchange, his increasing agitation with Melanie, finally, his barely controlled rage after the exchange. Yet, it's not clear how and if Louis is going to find release for that rage until he pulls the gun on Melanie. In the aftermath the violent outburst makes complete sense; full of pent-up anxiety, Louis was always a loaded gun waiting to go off.

De Niro's is a very satisfying performance to watch, because it allows, in fact demands the audience plays detective. In the lead-up to the shooting of Melanie, De Niro provides clues to what is about to happen in his muttered curses, his inability to complete a sentence, his pleading with Melanie to stop badgering him; and in his body language: the greased back hair, prison-style (dress code for some serious law breaking), the sweating, the nervous sideways glances, the facial contortions. Moreover, De Niro has also provided the background so that in hindsight the audience can deduce motive, which, in this case, is an expression of Louis' bad character, his background in violent crime and his history of being caught and locked up. In this sense, it's a generous performance too, because it invites the audience to participate, to fill in and flesh out the character of Louis.

In another interview, published in *Empire* magazine, Tarantino says: "From an acting standpoint, I'm as proud of Louis as any character I've ever written. As opposed to what people expect from my characters – great dialogue, great monologues – he doesn't have that. That's not who he is. It needs to come across through body language, by the way he sits in a chair. I remember describing to Robert that I saw his body language like a pile of dirty clothes. Well, I just happened to be talking to one of the greatest actors that has ever been produced when it comes to characterisation through body language, and he knew exactly what I was talking about."

In absence of dialogue and in view of Louis' inactivity, it's De Niro's body language that informs much of his performance in **Jackie Brown**. Louis' partial view of events, for example, is underlined by De Niro with a series of perplexed looks, glazed-over expressions and shrugs. There's a joke about Method acting, which refers, perhaps uncharitably, to De Niro's contemporary, Al Pacino and goes like this: During the course of working on a lavish period film about the American Revolution, the cast and crew come to a key scene in which the protagonist delivers a heart-felt speech, which encapsulates the essence of what the film is about – liberty, freedom, equality, etc. The film's star (Pacino) looks over his dialogue, then throws it aside, explaining to the director that he can say it all "with a look". De Niro does just this, but here it is in accordance with his director's intentions and is in no way egotistical – that being the point of the Pacino joke. Putting the humour aside, a facial expression, a mannerism, any minor movement delivered by these actors of the Method school, can and does speak volumes.

The third scene Louis appears in provides a good example of what De Niro achieves with looks, movements and mannerisms. Sent over to Simone's apartment by Ordell for a little R&R, Louis is treated to an eroticised karaoke performance, in which the woman mimes to The Supremes song, *Baby Love*. Sat stiff in the chair directly in front of Simone's gyrating body, Louis rocks back and forth, pats his hands on his thighs (out of time to the music) and stairs blankly ahead. Apart from giving the appearance of vacancy, ease, contentment, these few actions suggest a number of things: Louis is content with very little; satisfied with being anaesthetized (he spends much of the film getting high); prefers to watch, rather than participate; wants an easy life; lacks ambition and motivation; and is living in the past – signalled by his enjoyment of Motown music (evidenced by Simone's performance, but also a later conversation with Melanie about the Detroit disco scene). De Niro's performance suggests so much, so simply, in such "minor" scenes.

In terms of his interplay with the other actors, De Niro's performance

in **Jackie Brown** is probably the most generous of his career. With significantly less dialogue and action than the other members of the cast, much of his screen time amounts, technically speaking, to a series of reaction shots: a nod or shrug in response to a line of dialogue or a whole speech. For example, after being interrupting at Simone's apartment, Louis joins Ordell in the street where Beaumont's dead body is revealed in the trunk of Ordell's car. Louis asks who it is in the trunk, to which Ordell replies, "That's Beaumont." "Who's Beaumont?" says Louis. "An employee I had to let go", replies Ordell. Cut to Louis who registers mild surprise, checks the street around him and begins to display tentative curiosity. After explaining Beaumont's faults, Ordell invites Louis to work for him, saying: "If you're going to come in on this with me..." Cut once again to Louis who pats his moustache, folds his arms and clears his throat. In this scene it's Jackson who gets all the "cool" lines, closing with: "My nigger". Yet, the scene is as much De Niro's as it is Jackson's. Jackson has the dialogue, De Niro the body language – it becomes an equal screen partnership.

According to Tarantino, "The reason actors like to do my stuff is because they usually have a lot of cool things to say and they feel cool saying them." This is clearly not the case for De Niro in **Jackie Brown**; there's nothing cool about Louis Gara. Jackie Brown and Ordell Robbie are cool, as are Max Cherry and Melanie. Even the cops, Ray Nicolette and Mark Dargus, are cool in their own way. Just before shooting Louis, Ordell says with genuine regret, "What the fuck happened to you, man? Your ass used to be beautiful." Once again: Louis Gara is the odd character out, De Niro's is the odd performance out.

De Niro is an actor of monumental charisma. Since his early roles in Martin Scorsese films (**Mean Streets, Taxi Driver**), he has become a modern cinema icon. It's a status that dominates his performances. At times, his persona threatens to engulf his characters. Just how different, for example, are his goodfella, Jimmy Conway and casino mobster Ace Rothstein? They both display boyish grins and old men's scowls, as well as the trademark De Niro grimace and guffaw complete with inverted mouth smile. These are De Niro mannerisms turned into character traits and they remind us that we are always watching De Niro, the actor. Even playing a real-life person, Jake La Motta, the raging boxer who himself was larger than life, in and out of the ring, De Niro's persona punches through the performance. The opposite is true of his performance in **Jackie Brown**. Certainly, we are watching Robert De Niro/Louis Gara, simultaneously aware of both the actor's persona and the character's traits, but where De Niro inflates that persona as a goodfella or a boxing champ, in **Jackie Brown** he conflates his persona into the ex-con. That's perhaps as it should be; Conway and La Motta are grandstanding characters that demand a great deal of personal charisma. Louis Gara, on the other hand, is a small-time figure and so it's only appropriate that De Niro sublimate his persona for the role. That act is, in itself, a triumph of humility from one of the most famous actors on the planet, and singles out Louis Gara from the other characters in the Robert De Niro hall of fame.

A ROBERT DE NIRO
FILMOGRAPHY

Greetings (1968)
Sam's Song (aka Line Of Fire, 1969)
The Wedding Party (1969)
Bloody Mama (1970)
Hi, Mom! (aka Blue Manhattan, 1970)
Born To Win (aka Addict, 1971)
The Gang That Couldn't Shoot Straight (1971)
Jennifer On My Mind (1971)
Bang The Drum Slowly (1973)
Mean Streets (1973)
The Godfather: Part II (1974)
The Cinema According To Bertolucci (1975)
1900 (1976)
Taxi Driver (1976)
The Last Tycoon (1976)
New York, New York (1977)
The Deer Hunter (1978)
Raging Bull (1980)
True Confessions (1981)
The King of Comedy (1983)
Falling In Love (1984)
Once Upon A Time In America (1984)
Brazil (1985)
The Mission (1986)
The Untouchables (1987)
Angel Heart (1987)
Midnight Run (1988)
Jacknife (1989)
We're No Angels (1989)
GoodFellas (1990)
Stanley & Iris (1990)

Awakenings (1990)
Backdraft (1991)
Guilty By Suspicion (1991)
Cape Fear (1991)
Mistress (1992)
Night And The City (1992)
This Boy's Life (1993)
Mad Dog And Glory (1993)
A Bronx Tale (+ director, 1993)
Mary Shelley's Frankenstein (1994)
Heat (1995)
Casino (1995)
A Hundred And One Nights Of Simon Cinema (1995)
Marvin's Room (1996)
Sleepers (1996)
The Fan (1996)
Jackie Brown (1997)
Wag The Dog (1997)
Cop Land (1997)
A Salute To Martin Scorsese (1997, TV)
Great Expectations (1998)
New York City... Come Visit The World (1998)
Ronin (1998)
Flawless (1999)
Analyze This (1999)
15 Minutes (1999)
The Adventures Of Rocky And Bullwinkle (1999)

INDEX OF FILMS

Page number in bold indicates an illustration

www.creationbooks.com